An Improv State of Mind

using the art & science of improvisation
to succeed in business...and in life

Jennie Ayers

© 2014 by **BoldReads, a Division of BoldWork**

All Rights Reserved. No part of this publication may be reproduced in any form or by any means, including scanning, photocopying, or otherwise without prior written permission of the copyright holder.

First Printing, 2015

Printed in the United States of America

Library of Congress Cataloging-in-Publication Data
Ayers, Jennie
  An Improv State of Mind: using the art & science of
    improvisation to succeed in business…and in life
  ISBN 978-069 230 8226

For Kris

and to life…moment by moment

Contents

Forward………………………………………	i
Introduction………………………………	iv
An Improv State of Mind………………………………	1
Chapter One………………………………… The Case for Improvisation	4
Chapter Two ………………………………………… The Basics	9
Chapter Three ………………………………… Risk	17
Chapter Four …………………………… Ambiguity	25
Chapter Five ………………………………………. Flexibility & Adaptability	31
Chapter Six ………………………………………… Letting Go & Accepting from Others – The Art of Collaboration	35
Chapter Seven ………………………………….. Listening – The Bedrock of Communication	45
Chapter Eight …………………………… Creativity	57

Chapter Nine .... Before We Begin	68
Glossary of Improv Terms	75
The 5 Stages of Improvisation	77
The Games	79

Warm Ups
Warm Up #1, Ask a Silly Question.....................	85
Warm Up #2, Pass the Frog	88
Warm Up #3, Keep It Up!	91
Warm Up #4, Sound Circle	94
Warm Up #5, Barney	97

Beyond the Warm Up
The Alphabet Story	100
Sixty Second Life	103
A Change of Hat	105
Rescue Me	108
Lines from a Hat	111
Conducted Story	114
Draw Person aka Paired Drawing	117
Goal on One Side	119
What's on Your List?	122
The Way I See It	125
This is not a Rope	128
Sell This aka Spontaneous Marketing	130
Innovate or Die	133
Yes, And	136
Add a Word aka One Word at a Time	139
Awareness Quiz	142
Tag-a-Word	145

Say What? ……………………………………… 147
Carpooling ……………………………………..… 150

The Yada, Yada, Yada Interview
    aka Gibberish Interview …….....… 153
Sculpt This! ………..………………..…… 156
Stop Action ……………...……………..…… 159

Status Games

    Demonstrate Status ………………………… 163
    Pecking Order …………………………… 167
    Card Status ……………………………… 170

Additional Resources …………………………….. 173

End Notes ……………………………………. 174

Bibliography …………………………………….. 176

Foreword
By Rebecca Ripley
Author of *Managing by Thinking Around; Leadership Coaching – The Fast Track to Effectiveness (with Kittie Watson and Barbara Braham)* and the American Management Association's First Creativity and Innovation Workshop

With *An Improv State of Mind*, Jennie Ayers has filled a gap in the world of corporate creativity and innovation. This Field Guide will be a resource to new and seasoned facilitators, coaches and leaders alike as they strive to tap into the latent creative potential that resides within all participants.

Given the author's prior life as a Hollywood comedy writer, it's no surprise that her style is both entertaining and compelling. The book provides an array of engaging experiences that are clearly described and ready to implement. Every reader is sure to find numerous activities that will help participants "get outside their heads" and into a playful, spontaneous, yet focused creative space. Jennie includes useful reminders and provocative debrief questions to pave the way for successful implementation.

In addition to many fun, practical warm-ups and games and fresh perspective on classic topics such as listening, change and ambiguity, Jennie includes a synopsis of relevant research and a brief history of improvisation. This introduction provides the foundation many of us need to feel grounded when trying new approaches. She helps us see that improvisation goes way beyond comedy sketches. It is simply a powerful technique that transitions participants into a supportive, judgment-free zone for discovery.

And as Jennie says, "Through improvisation, we can get to the point where it's easy to come up with a dozen reasons why an idea will work." And in today's business climate, we want to live in the land of 'why this idea will work'. Dig in and enjoy. You'll be glad you did!

To the Moment!
Rebecca Ripley
Columbia, MD
2014

About the Author

Jennie Ayers, Senior Partner with **BoldWork**, is an experienced and certified coach specializing in building more effective influence, leadership and communication skills, while focusing on creating and sustaining health work environments. Much of her work focuses on issues relative to how we engage with others and alter our behavior to positively impact interpersonal effectiveness and build effective collaborative teams.

She uses her expertise in improvisation to hone the skill of improvisational thinking and to strengthen creativity, adaptability and spontaneous communication.

Jennie is a former actor, producer and director in theatre, and spent almost 20 years as a TV comedy writer, including two years writing for comic Jeff Foxworthy.

Introduction

I was still fairly new to writing television comedy when my partner Susan Sebastian and I got a pitch meeting at Paramount Studios for the show "Dear John." The show starred Judd Hirsch (from "Taxi" fame) as easygoing John Lacey whose wife dumps him for his best friend. John joins a self-help group for divorced, widowed and lonely people. A key member of the group is Kirk Morris, a cocky ladies man, played by Jere Burns. (You may know him as Wynn Duffy on "Justified.")

We were freelancers at the time, meaning that we hadn't landed a full time writing gig on a show's staff. Our agent was sending spec scripts to shows he thought we'd be right for and if the powers that be liked what they read, they'd invite us to come in and pitch ideas for an episode of their show. Because those freelance assignments often led to a staff job, we felt the pressure to make every pitch count.

We went in to "Dear John" with what we thought were six dynamite ideas. Before we knew it, the guy hearing our pitch was standing up and thanking us for coming in…one of the more polite ways we'd been told "No Sale" in Hollywood. I felt like I was walking the last mile as I moved toward the door to leave. The guy's on my heels, ready to close his office door in my face and on my dreams when I suddenly blurt out, "John gets paid for sex and feels dirty." Silence…for an eternity. And then he smiles and says, "That could be funny." He wants to hear more.

Susan and I sat back down to wing it. We made up a story about how Kirk sets John up with a blind date who turns out to be a very attractive professional woman who's in town for a conference. She and John hit it off and he ends up going back to her hotel room, where he wakes up the next morning to find her dressed, off to catch an early plane. She tells John the evening was fabulous and she'll call him the next time she's in town. "Can you be available?" Of course he can. He likes this woman…a lot. She tells him to take his time, have a bubble bath, check out time is noon. She kisses him, puts money on the nightstand and is off, leaving our main character feeling used and dirty. (By the way, Judd Hirsch was fabulous; he made the funny in the scene real and touching.) When John complains to Kirk about what happened, Kirk fesses up that he's been working as a paid escort and John's "date" thought he did the same thing. It was all a misunderstanding, although Kirk says he's never stooped so low as to charge a client for his favors.

We got the freelance assignment. In fact, that episode opened the show's third season and we went on to write two more episodes that same season.

And this all happened because my partner and I had the ability to come up with a new idea "in the moment." We improvised.

I know what you're thinking. "I can't do that."

Yes you can. There's no mystery to being able to "think on your feet" or respond to whatever's coming at you "in the moment." It's a skill you can learn.

And I'm going to help you.

An Improv State of Mind

The skills we need in business today are forcing us to look outside traditional "training" methods. You might not be thinking about improvisation, but I bet you *are* thinking, "How do I get my team to share ideas and collaborate more effectively?" "How do we innovate?" "How do we come up with the best solutions to challenging problems?" "How do we stay productive in the face of change?"

Improvisation was invaluable to me as a performer and a writer, but it was BoldWork's managing partner, Kris Campbell, who first wondered aloud if improvisation would be useful in her work in leadership development to build those competencies that are intangible.

The answer, of course, is yes. And we've introduced the practice of improvisation to many of our business clients with much success.

While I use the term "coach" or "facilitator" throughout simply because it's easy, this Field Guide is written for the improv novice as well as for coaches, trainers, facilitators, talent managers, teachers, team leaders, OD professionals, people in sales – anyone who is ready to embrace new ways to learn and wants to use improvisation effectively in their business and their life. As a tool, improvisation provides the opportunity to sharpen a variety of skills all at once.

It helps us challenge our habitual ways of thinking and behaving to become more flexible and adaptable. It can help us be more effective when working in an environment that's ambiguous - we have to continue to move forward even when we're unsure of what lies ahead. Improvisation arouses and strengthens our long-buried creativity. It reinforces the importance of collaboration and teamwork. It enhances our ability to tune in to our environment and stay "in the moment" to make sure that we accurately interpret the verbal and non-verbal cues we pick up, which makes us more effective communicators. And it builds self-confidence so that we can once again trust ourselves and bank on our own instincts.

There are those in business today who tout improvisation as the next "killer app"…because it's perfect for leaders, aspiring leaders, trainers, coaches, facilitators, teachers, designers, project managers….anyone faced with situations where real time execution means the difference between success and failure.

Intrigued…but not sure where to start?

Just be open to what's about to come at you….and turn the page.

"Improvisation is a wonderful example of the kind of thinking 'blink' is about. Improvisation involves people making very sophisticated decisions in the spur of the moment."
Malcolm Gladwell, author, "blink: The Power of Thinking without Thinking"

"Improvisation isn't about comedy. It's about reacting – being focused and present in the moment at a very high level."
Robert Kulhan, Duke University's Fuqua School of Business

"Every organization must have the flexibility to listen to the marketplace, learn from their customers and make changes when appropriate. To accomplish this, companies should treat strategy as 'improvisational theatre'."
Rosabeth Moss Kanter, Harvard School of Business

Chapter One
The Case for Improvisation

If you're already hooked on the idea of using improvisation in business, you might skip this section. If you haven't fully made the connection between improv and the workplace, please read on.

So Long Industrial Age, Hello Knowledge Era

If we look at how we do business today – and what we value – we see that a lot has changed. For the better part of the last hundred years, our country's wealth came from industry, from things we built, things we could hold in our hand. We measured a company's value in tangibles – their factories, their inventory. Yet even as early as the 1950's, Peter Drucker – the man who invented management as a field of study and coined the phrase "knowledge work" – was looking at workers and how they needed to be managed differently.

Today, we've moved full force from the Industrial Age into the Knowledge Era, where we measure a company's value in intangibles – by the knowledge of its workers, and how these workers are able to share and recombine that collective knowledge and invest it in their organizations. Knowledge is the new currency that gives companies their competitive edge.

This Knowledge Era asks more from each one of us, both as leaders and workers. We have to be willing to replace self-interest with doing what's best for the whole, which means having the ability to share what we know with others and to recombine that knowledge into new knowledge. Edward O. Wilson refers to this unity of knowledge as consilence. [1]

In this Knowledge Era, the lines between leader and worker blur. A command-and-control leadership style is out and a more collaborative leadership style is in. Leaders no longer have the luxury of control but instead have to focus on creating healthy work environments where everyone contributes and does their best work. Effective leaders need effective teams.

Idea-generation (to have as many ideas as possible) takes precedence over idea-geography (ideas must come from the leader). Everyone, no matter where they are in an organization's hierarchy, needs to be willing and able to contribute new ideas, new ways of thinking and doing, and be willing to accept and build on the ideas of others. With the entrance of Gen Y's (aka Millenials) into the workplace, the traditional view of top-down management is being challenged. That's not going to change as the newest generation – Gen 2020s or linksters – begins entering the workforce.

New Skills for a New Era

We need new skills for this Knowledge Era. To stay competitive, organizations and their workforce need the flexibility and adaptability to respond quickly and effectively to a changing marketplace and economy. As Malcolm Gladwell says in "blink: The Power of Thinking without Thinking,"[2] "people need to be able to make very sophisticated decisions on the spur of the moment." Leaders have to be willing to make these decisions in times that are often ambiguous and risky.

Today's business professionals need to be adept at seeing a situation from different perspectives. What worked yesterday won't necessarily work today and what works today may very well not work tomorrow. Innovation is key and creativity is the bridge to innovation. Not only do leaders have to awaken their own intrinsic creativity, they have to create and sustain the kind of healthy work climate where an entire work force is encouraged to be creative and innovative.

Harvard Business Professor Rosabeth Moss Kanter puts it well when she says that business today is less a results oriented process than it is "an imaginative exercise."[3] She envisions that creativity is like looking at the world through a kaleidoscope. You look at a set of elements, the same ones everyone else sees, but then you reassemble those floating bits and pieces into an interesting new possibility. That's what effective leaders are able to do.

Also foundational to being successful today is the skill to be an effective communicator, which carries with it a changed definition of "good communication." It's no longer enough to be an attentive listener, check for feedback and stay engaged. We now must possess social awareness and social facility. Simply put, we need to be empathetic (and accurate in our empathy), have social cognition (understand how the world works) and be confident in our ability to influence and self-present.

So...what's the prognosis for our future workforce? Well, when it comes to having the skills they need to compete in today's market, future workers get an F. According to a 2006 study, "Are They Really Ready to Work?", a vast majority of students simply don't acquire the skills they need in either high school or college, which means that companies have to provide learning experiences to develop those skills. And a 2014 Gallup poll revealed that only 11 percent of business leaders think that new college graduates have the necessary skills and competencies to succeed in today's workplace. [4]

Turns out our current workforce isn't faring much better. According to the Institute for Corporate Productivity's 2013 Global Leadership Development Survey, specific competencies that people need to succeed today – like creativity and innovation - simply aren't being addressed. [5]

It all sounds overwhelming, doesn't it? How do we prepare our workforce – how do we prepare ourselves – for the challenges in this fast-changing, global economy?

Take a deep breath. Exhale. If you need to take another breath, go ahead. I'll wait.

The bottom line? There are many ways you can learn and/or hone the skills you'll need to succeed in 21st century business. (These same skills will help you succeed in life as well.)

And one of the very best is through improvisation.

Chapter Two

The Basics

Improvisation – What Is It?

When most people hear the word "improvisation", they think of people making up funny skits or television shows like "Saturday Night Live," since so many of this show's performers come from the world of improvisation. But improvisation goes back much further – it predates writing. Long before we wrote down our stories, we acted them out.

During grad school, I was a teaching assistant for a class in theatre history that spanned the years 500 BC to 1642. I fell in love with the Commedia Dell'Arte. In the mid-1500's, groups of roving comic performers traveled from town to town throughout Europe. They didn't rely on a formal script, but rather loose scenarios which set out the broad strokes of how to enter and exit and who would play what character. Otherwise, the players made up dialogue and action as the story unfolded. The troupe would often skewer current politicians. (Early satire.) This was early improvisation.

We trace modern improvisation to Viola Spolin, who worked with immigrant children in her role as a recreational director for the city of Chicago. She used theatre games in the late 1930's to help immigrant children socially integrate and adapted these games for the WPA. (Works Progress Administration was the largest of Roosevelt's New Deal agencies. It employed millions to carry out public works projects and operate arts, drama, media and literacy projects.) Spolin further refined these games to focus on creativity and play, to help people get in touch with their own ability to be creative.

"…perceiving trumps preconception."

In the early 1950's, Spolin's son, Paul Sills, co-founded a theatre group which expanded on many of his mother's methods (as well as created new ones). This group eventually evolved into Second City; the number of performers who came to prominence via that venue is legendary (Tina Fey, Amy Poehler, Gilda Radner, Bill Murray, Dan Ackroyd, Julia-Louis Dreyfuss, Jane Lynch, Steve Carrell, Mike Myers and Martin Short to name just a few.)

Paralleling what was going on in America, Englishman Keith Johnstone was developing his own theories about spontaneity and creativity in theatre. He invented the improv form known as Theatresports and addressed the concepts of blocking and status, which are so important in today's practice of improvisation. Status games can be especially useful in multi-generational workplaces. (More on this later.)

Whether improvisation took place in the 16th Century or last week on TV, its goal remains the same. To create stories spontaneously in a supportive and judgment-free atmosphere. Participants are encouraged to explore all that's possible, knowing that in improvisation, there are no wrong answers, just opportunities for discovery.

The POC – Bedrock of Improv

In her book, "Improvisation for the Theatre," Viola Spolin introduces the concept of Point of Concentration (POC), the bedrock upon which modern improvisation is built. The POC is simply the focal point of each game. Think of it in terms of a soccer game. The POC of the game is the ball. Players, individually and collectively as a team, must focus on the ball. And they do so, having no idea how the game is going to turn out.

It's not unusual to lose sight of this POC, especially when you're working with people new to improvisation. It's okay (even preferable) to stop an exercise and ask everyone to refocus.

Spolin advocates that the same singleness of focus in improvisation frees the participants to act spontaneously and provides a vehicle for an organic rather than cerebral experience. In other words, players "get outside their heads." In improvisation, perceiving trumps preconception.

Take a minute and think about that. How much more effective might we be if we could operate with full hearts and full minds "in the moment" rather than expending energy on trying to figure out and deal with "things that might be"?

It's No Free-for-All

Improvisation is no free-for-all, with players doing whatever they want, with no regard for their co-players. In fact, one of the primary goals in improv is to make our fellow players look good. Every improvisational game has a framework in which the players operate. The Point of Concentration sets the rules of the game – it's the thing that's to be done.

Take the example of a game called "Pass the Frog."(page 86) [Note: The same improvisational game may be known by more than one name. I use the names familiar to me.]

Players stand in a circle. The player who is "it" must list as many items as s/he can in a certain category (say state capitals) as a stuffed frog is passed completely around the circle. The goal of the exercise is to concentrate and focus under pressure. The POC is the naming of the state capitals. If the participant starts naming presidents, s/he is outside the POC. As a facilitator, this is when you would stop the game and remind everyone what the Point of Concentration is.

Improvisation is Not Performing

The concept of "performing" implies planning. Musicians and singers rehearse songs and determine a play list. Actors learn dialogue and have run thrus. Even stand ups try out material in smaller venues to see which jokes fly and which fall flat. Across the board, performers plan "how" they're going to do something.

In improvisation, there is no "how" because we have no idea what we'll be doing until the moment we start to do it. Improvisation creates reality "in the moment."

While improvisation isn't about performing, we can certainly acknowledge that it's entertaining. When we buy a ticket to see an improv troupe, we expect to be entertained. When we're using improvisation as a tool to build skills, however, entertainment's not what we're after…although it's often a natural by-product. As a facilitator, if you see participants trying to entertain the group rather than concentrate on building skills, it's helpful to stop and revisit the purpose of the game.

> *"…(there's a) need to prepare for unpredictability."*

Tina Fey Need Not Apply

Improvisation isn't about being funny. Business professionals need to be reassured that they're not expected to be the next Tina Fey, Stephen Colbert, Jon Stewart, Jimmy Fallon, Wanda Sykes or whoever's hot right now.

The biggest belly laughs come from our everyday lives, when we discover the gaps between what we expect something or someone to be like and the reality of what or who they are. Some improvisations turn out to be funny, simply because the unexpected happens.

I remember playing "Pass the Frog" with a group of employees from a financial institution. As you might guess, many of them had little experience getting up in front of co-workers and had a certain level of discomfort, wondering if they would be competent when it was their "turn." It's not unusual for people who haven't had much experience with improvisation to be uncomfortable at first. They may feel self-conscious, worried that they won't do well in front of others. It helps to acknowledge the feelings as perfectly normal and reassure people that they don't have to take part if they don't want to.

> *"Try a warm up or two to get people comfortable."*

One woman appeared to be so shy that I wasn't sure she'd join in. But she was a trooper and when it was her turn, she was asked to name as many words as she could that begin with the letter "L". As the frog made its way around the circle, the first words she uttered were "liquor," "lingerie," "leather" and "lust." The entire group broke out in laughter, perhaps seeing a side of a fellow employee they hadn't known existed. That laughter broke the ice and bolstered the congeniality of the group.

That experience helps remind us that even though *improvisation isn't about being funny, it is about having fun.*

Getting Started

Always keep in mind that your goal is to provide an environment in which participants can learn to think more improvisationally and apply the skills learned and strengthened during the games to their everyday work life. You're not trying to turn out actors proficient in improvisation.

There are going to be people who are enthusiastic and embrace the concepts and validity of using improvisational thinking in business immediately. There are also going to be those who don't, at first, see its relevance. Be patient. Invite people to participate. If someone refuses to take part, that's okay. They can just watch. (In all the time I've been using improv in business, I've only had one person who refused to join in.)

It helps to provide some background on improvisation (though not too much talk – improv is about doing). Lend credibility to its use by letting participants know that business schools like Harvard, Stanford and MIT have improvisation as part of their curriculum and that major companies use it to help hone leadership skills and build more collaborative teams all across their organizations. Even some medical schools are now offering improv classes to their students, as it helps to improve communication, cognition and teamwork. Turns out that physicians and improvisers face the same paradox – the need to prepare for unpredictability.

Introduce participants to the language of improvisation. I've included a short list of terms used in teaching and practicing improvisation (pages 73-74) so participants are clear on what they're being asked to do and can use a common language when they talk about their observations and experiences of a particular game. I'm also including a list of what I call the "Five Stages of Improvisation" (page 75) to help you understand a participant's level of engagement during the game.

Debriefing each game is key. It gives participants the opportunity to make the connection between the game and the skills the game builds, and how these skills are relevant and applicable to their everyday work lives.

Before you plunge into a whole day of improvisation, introduce it in small doses. Try a warm up or two to get people comfortable with experimenting and then build on those experiences.

Be patient. Be supportive. Improvise!

Chapter Three

Risk

> *"Don't be afraid to go out on a limb. That's where the fruit is."*
> H. Jackson Browne

I love that quote! We should all be reaching for the fruit in life!

Risk…to try something new when the outcome is unknown.

Not so long ago, the mantle of being a risk taker rested clearly on the shoulders of the entrepreneur. Not anymore. Business today is complex and constantly changing. Everyone – no matter where we are in an organization, be it leader or worker – has to be entrepreneurial in spirit. That means all of us have to be willing to take risks in order to succeed. You remember the saying, "Nothing ventured, nothing gained?" That couldn't be truer for those in business today.

Nike's iconic call to "Just Do It!" could be the new global mantra as companies are challenged to let go of habitual ways of thinking and doing and embrace new ways to manage complex change and the amount of information native to the Knowledge Era. Navigating today's business world is like riding white water rapids – it's fast and it's full of surprises.

But if taking risks is vital to a company's success, why are so few in business willing to take them?

Fear.

Fear as Motivator? Not!

One of my favorite books is by Jeffrey Pfeffer and Robert I. Sutton - "The Knowing-Doing Gap: How Smart Companies Turn Knowledge into Action." The authors confront the challenge of taking what we know is required to improve performance and turning that knowledge into action. For example, we know that fear isn't an effective way to manage or lead. It actually undermines employee performance. Fear builds barriers and makes us more guarded, unwilling to share. And yet, there are still people who use fear in order to get employees to do what they want.

People and companies who have a history of "punishing ideas" and leading through fear crush the spirit of risk.

> *"What we learn during the process of putting ideas together can be as valuable as the idea itself."*

Soft Landings

Thankfully, not all companies respond to the failure of an idea harshly. Pfeffer and Sutton also talk about "soft landings" in their book and offer the following example about Thomas Watson, Sr., IBM's founder and CEO for many decades:

> A promising junior executive of IBM was involved in a risky venture for the company and managed to lose over $10 million in the gamble. It was a disaster. When Watson called the nervous executive into his office, the young man blurted out, "I guess you want my resignation." Watson replied, "You can't be serious. We just spent $10 million educating you!"[6]

(A fellow said he was told this same story by the Manager of Human Resources when IBM hired him in 1974, right out of college. He said it reflected what he came to admire as IBM's approach to failure – that it could and should be turned into a learning experience.)

Companies that embrace "soft landings" realize what those who practice improvisation realize – that what we learn during the process of putting ideas into action can be as valuable as the idea itself. Improvisation – and "soft landings" - turn the concept of "failure" on its ear.

Even those companies that embrace a "culture of forgiveness" can expect a work force to offer some resistance, simply because it is entrenched in habitual ways of thinking and doing.

During our climate work with a major health care company, the new COO brought in to affect a turnaround in the company's bottom line openly sought input and new ideas from her executive team. Not one of them would risk speaking up, in spite of repeated assurances that there would be no backlash, no "punishing of ideas". We used an exercise called "Sixty Second Life" (page 101) to provide a safe arena where team members could take the initial risk to speak up. We then introduced "The Way I See It" (page 123) which encouraged them to imagine what their ideal work environment would be. With patience, team members transferred their ability to speak up during the improv games to speaking up during meetings. Over time, the team's dynamic shifted. Members became more trusting, more confident in one another and better collaborators. This new team dynamic helped make the work climate much healthier.

Being Cast Out by the Tribe

Fear of reprisal isn't the only thing that stops us from being risk takers. We know from research into human behavior that all of us need to feel competent in our work. And we need to feel like the people we work with see us as competent. If we think we're perceived as incompetent, we "lose face" and we're just not willing to take risks for fear of losing face or looking foolish in front of our coworkers. Again, this fear of being incompetent contributes to a toxic work climate.

As kids, most of us can remember doing something totally crazy because someone dared us to do it and we didn't want to be labeled a "chicken" and shunned by our friends. Once we're in the work force, we have that same primal desire to stay part of the tribe, only now we <u>don't</u> do something (like take a risk) in order to remain part of the group. Once we act outside our company's norms (even if we've been given permission by the company to do so), we don't know how others will perceive us and it's safer just to "color inside the lines." This can be especially true if the culture of the company is affiliative (based on relationships and personal networks). Our co-workers become our friends. We're all part of the same tribe. When we alter our behavior and become different from the rest of the tribe, we risk being cast out.

I'm Only One Person

The other fear that keeps us from taking risks is the fear that we'll prove our own insignificance. How many times have you heard someone say, "What can I do? I'm only one person." Many people feel insignificant, both at work and in their personal lives. They can't imagine how what they think matters to their company and they can't conceive how one person could possibly influence its overall success or failure. Feeling insignificant reinforces our reluctance to step forward, speak out and take a risk. If we do, and what we offer appears not to make a difference, doesn't that prove how insignificant we are?

Improvisation – From Reluctance to Willingness

If we believe that taking risks is vital to succeed in the Knowledge Era, how do we transform people unwilling to take risks into people willing to take them? We do two things – address their fears and make individuals feels significant. Improvisation does both.

Another View of Failure

> "I make more mistakes than anyone else I know, and sooner or later, I patent most of them."[7]   Thomas Edison

Remember that one reason people don't take risks is their fear of failure. By its very nature, improvisation is unpredictable. A story may start off in one direction and veer off in another. But instead of seeing that shift as a failure to reach the original goal, what if we see it as an opportunity to discover something new?

Imagine the things we've discovered on the road to "failure." Both Silly Putty and Scotch guard were created when things went wrong while chemists were trying to create synthetic rubber. Post-It-Notes came about because the glue 3M was trying to make simply wasn't strong enough. The microwave oven was invented by accident when Percy Spencer discovered that his chocolate bar had melted when he accidentally left it too close to an experiment he was running on radar systems.[8] And Cinderella's original fur shoe turned into a glass slipper when a Frenchman was writing down the fairy tale as it was being told to him and he confused one homonym (vair, meaning fur) with another homonym (verre, meaning glass).[9]

What about our fear of "losing face", of appearing incompetent in front of our co-workers? As improvisers, we embrace and celebrate improv's golden rule – "yes and" – knowing that any offer (that's the dialogue or action which advances a story) will be accepted. Improvisation is free of judgment. There is no "losing face" because there is no right or wrong.

One Person Can Make a Difference

And what about our feelings of insignificance? There's a principle in improvisation, "bring a brick, not a cathedral." I can't remember when I first heard that phrase, but I've never come across a better explanation of it than the one offered by Tom Yorton, President of Second City Communications, in his article "Using Improv Methods to Overcome the Fear Factor".

> "First, seemingly small contributions matter a great deal to the whole. On stage, a simple shoulder shrug or pregnant pause can make or break a scene and it can be as important as all the previous action…combined. Second, this axiom underscores the idea that the whole is greater than the sum of its parts."[10]

In games like "The Alphabet Story" (page 98) and "Add a Word" (page 137), everyone has to contribute in order to tell a story. And it's this same notion – that everyone's contribution matters – that applies to our work lives and can help people understand how their individual contributions are meaningful to the company as a whole. Once people believe they have something worthwhile to offer, they're more likely to risk speaking out.

Services and information are supplanting industry and goods. Our country's major opportunity for success in the foreseeable future lies in the formulation and exportation of new ideas. Companies will find success by having workers who aren't afraid to risk sharing knowledge and contribute these new ideas.

"Managing ambiguity is that tension between rushing to the clear, the concrete and managing this ambiguous fuzzy area in the middle. Managing ambiguity is something we have to teach because we have to counter the story of a single linear solution."[11]
Professor Helen Haste, Harvard

Chapter Four
Ambiguity

"Life is about not knowing, having to change, taking the moment and making the best of it, without knowing what's going to happen next. Delicious ambiguity."[12]
Gilda Radner

Ambiguity – uncertain, unclear, open to or having several possible meanings

I was watching an old sci fi movie not long ago – one of those really awful ones done on the cheap in the days before sophisticated computer generated images. A young guy's fleeing some kind of mutated monster by running through a huge pipe that's supposed to be part of the vast sewer system of a big city. Suddenly, he runs out of pipe and finds himself standing on the edge of the opening to the pipe, looking down into a black hole. Tacky sound effects and music – we know the monster's coming. He looks down at the black hole and debates whether or not to jump. The music gets louder to let us know that the monster's getting closer. The guy looks in the direction of the approaching monster, then back at the hole. Jump! He turns back to the monster just in time to see it come at him. Jump! The guy freezes, unable to move. The monster devours him.

The Need for "Cognitive Closure"

I know what you're thinking. It was a movie. In real life, the guy would have jumped. But would he? Not necessarily. According to social psychologists, people want firm answers to their questions and have an aversion toward ambiguity. It's what they call a need for "cognitive closure".

> *"We depend on precedent, when what we need is fresh thinking...."*

The guy in the movie had a question about that black hole, "What's down there?" The answer was ambiguous, "Don't know." Our movie character froze, unable to take the action needed to save his life, because he was moving from something he knew (the approaching monster) to something unknown (the black hole).

That same reluctance to move forward in the face of ambiguity also happens in business. And that reluctance can be costly. Our need for closure too often causes us to rely on things we already know or actions we've taken in the past. We depend on precedent when what we need is fresh thinking and a new approach to challenge.

A Knowledge Driven Economy

The way we do business today isn't the same way we did business fifty years ago, twenty years ago, even five years ago. We live and work in a global society of rapid change. We don't have the luxury of analyzing every detail before we make decisions. We live in a knowledge driven economy and, as Michael Rosenberg says in his book, "The Flexible Thinker: A Guide to Creative Wealth", we can't possibly know all the facts.[13] Yet we still have to make decisions and move forward. In other words, we have to be able to tolerate a certain amount of ambiguity and continue to act with self-confidence.

No "Do Overs"

At its core, the practice of improvisation is built on ambiguity. An exercise or "game" is open to several possibilities, dependent only upon the direction its players take it. A game like "Conducted Story" (page 112) asks participants to create a single story even as one player is cut off and another is asked to step in. The game, like improvisation itself, forces us to give up control over where we are going and instead pay attention to the journey as we experience it. There's no planning ahead and we're expected to drive on, even though we don't know exactly where we're going to end up.

Through improvisation, we learn how not to freeze in the face of ambiguity but push through it. During an improv exercise, we don't have time to evaluate all options but instead must rely on taking action based on limited information. We make decisions on how to move forward with no chance for a "do over."

Plan Less, Discover More

Tom Yorton writes about an interesting notion: plan less and discover more.[14] That's the very essence of improvisation. My former writing partner and I put that notion to the test often during our career and were rewarded for it.

When you write on staff for a television sit com, you usually come up with an idea for a script and then get together with the whole staff to "beat out" the story. Then you go off and write an outline.

The outline details what happens in the story and how the characters act and react. It also tracks the characters' emotional arcs (what the characters go through emotionally throughout the story).

After the outline gets approved, you get sent off to write the script. My partner and I sometimes wrote together and sometimes separately. When we wrote separately, we'd each take the outline and bang out our version of the script. Then we'd come together, compare the two and take the best stuff from each script.

There were times, however, when we couldn't do that because one of us had abandoned the outline and stepped off the abyss into uncertain terrain. Instead of following the story we'd gotten approved, we let our characters explore alternative paths, often with no clear idea of where they were headed. We let our characters move forward in ambiguity. And in doing that, we often discovered things about the character we hadn't thought of before and the scripts were always better because of those discoveries.

"Staying Open"

In workshops, when I ask people to tell me the first word that pops into their head when I say "ambiguity", I usually get some variation of the following:
- Chaos
- Confusion
- Scary
- Unknown
- Unclear

All of those words have a negative connotation. Improvisation helps us experience the positive side of ambiguity. Ambiguity allows us to stay open. It invites us to let go of habitual ways of thinking and doing and embrace new possibilities.

Brian Tate, creativity facilitator for the Leading Teams High Performance program at the Banff Center, says, "The thing we're least tolerant of is ambiguity. If we get used to the discomfort…it will emerge into something else. Success with change comes from how willing we are to hang out in ambiguity."[15]

In today's climate of quick change, we have to be willing to "hang out in ambiguity." And we need to change the way we perceive or think about ambiguity – not as something chaotic or unclear – but as something having several possible meanings. The practice of improvisation provides us with a safe place to learn how to change.

"Being adaptable in a global playing field will be one of the most important assets any worker can have."[16]
       Thomas L. Friedman

Chapter Five
Flexibility & Adaptability

So Long, Schwinn

As a kid, I rode a bright blue Schwinn bicycle. I loved that bike. It was freedom. All of my friends had Schwinn bicycles. Through the 1970's, this family-owned company was America's number one manufacturer of bicycles. But by the 1980's, the trend in biking had shifted to motocross and mountain bikes. And adults were shelling out big bucks for upscale, lightweight bicycles they could take anywhere. Top management at Schwinn failed to adapt to the change in what riders wanted and eventually went belly up in 1992, filing for bankruptcy.[17]

In today's business climate, the only constant is change. And the ability of a company to navigate change, to manage it successfully, rests on the capability of its workers to be both flexible and adaptable.

First-Order Change

People often use the words "flexible" and "adaptable" interchangeably, as if they mean the same thing. They don't.

In business, we associate flexibility with first-order change. First-order change simply means doing more or less of something that we're already doing. For example, say your company moves from a five day, 40 hour work week to a four day, 40 hour work week. This is first-order change. The structure of your company's work force remains basically constant, except that you and other workers now go into the office four days each week instead of five. You accommodate that new schedule by being *flexible*.

Second-Order Change

But let's say that your company abandons a structured work week altogether. Everybody's now going to telecommute. They'll no longer be required or encouraged to come into the office on a regular basis and it will be up to everyone to set their own hours – what days they'll work, how many hours each day, etc.

The company has transformed itself from a traditional employer with an on-site work force to an entrepreneurial organization. This kind of transformation is recognized as second-order change.

Now, in order to accommodate this transformation, everyone in the work force is going to have to alter habitual ways of thinking about work (it's a 40 hour week and they go on-site to perform their jobs). They'll have to abandon fundamental beliefs about work (that it requires external structure) and embrace new ways of thinking about it (it can be done anywhere, at any time). In other words, they'll have to *adapt* to this new structure. Second order change often requires new knowledge and skills to implement and can conflict with a person's ingrained values and/or norms...which is why second order change so often fails.

Improv Newbies Show Flexibility

Now most business professionals, when first asked to experiment with improvisation, feel anxious. That's not surprising. After all, improvisation is open-ended. It asks us to stay open to all possibilities. That's outside the comfort zone of most people in business – we know through research that 75% of those in business seek structure and closure. But most people are at least willing to give improvisation a try. And the moment they agree to take part in an improv game, they exhibit flexibility! Congratulations. For example, a game like "What's on Your List?" (page 120) both encourages flexible thinking and requires letting go of preconceived ideas.

> *"We have to let go of habitual ways of thinking....."*

Moving from Flexibility to Adaptability

It's one thing to experiment with improvisation on a casual basis. But to fully embrace it, we have to let go of habitual ways of thinking and doing and *adapt* to improvisation's inherently changing nature. We have to let go of the concept of closure because, in improvisation, we have no idea where a game will take us. We can't anticipate where it's going or how it will end because the game is in the collective hands of all the participants. Improvisation asks us to be spontaneous, to "think on our feet" and respond to whatever's thrown at us.

The more we practice improvisation, however, the more comfortable we become with its open-ended process. It's like taking someone who is naturally right-handed and asking them to only use their left hand. It's awkward and uncomfortable at first. But we know with practice. this person can learn to use their left hand as easily as their right In other words, they learn to *adapt*.

We can all learn to adapt.

From Anxiety to Anticipation

Because improvisation is constantly changing, it forces us to break old patterns of both thought and behavior. Once we break these patterns, we can begin to see new possibilities in old information. We begin to learn to create order out of chaos and to trust our instincts. Improvisation helps us move from the "anxiety of surprise" to the "anticipation of surprise."

Chapter Six
Letting Go & Accepting from Others – The Art of Collaboration

Holding On to the Familiar

Hollywood executives are programmed to say no. At least, that's what Dan Taradash told me over coffee one day. I had the great good fortune to meet this talented, generous and decent man when I was just beginning my career as a television writer and he was coming to the end of his illustrious career as a screenwriter. Dan won an Academy Award for "From Here to Eternity" and wrote or co-wrote several other films, including "Golden Boy", "Bell, Book and Candle", "Picnic", "Hawaii", "Knock on Any Door" and a dozen others. Dan's pronouncement proved especially prophetic when my writing partner and I started pitching series ideas.

We considered our ideas new, original, fresh. Unfortunately for us, Hollywood wasn't looking for ideas that were new, original or fresh, even though they said that's exactly what they were looking for. The truth is, Hollywood looks for shows that sound like shows that have already been successful. So we gave in to the reality and started to pitch ideas with that in mind. As an example, I'd always wanted to do a comedy about what it's like to grow up fat in America. Nobody would touch it but when we started pitching it as the Brady Bunch with a fat Marcia, we were suddenly taking meetings on it (even though the Brady Bunch had been off the air for more than 2 decades). Hollywood's resistance to new also accounts for the high number of sequels.

Too often, businesses are like Hollywood. They rely on what's familiar. Or, as Pfeffer and Sutton refer to it, organizations can "use memory as a substitute for thinking" and do what's "always been done without reflecting." [18]

Too many organizations continue to operate this way, even though it's not beneficial to the company. Given the nature of business today, and the rapidly changing environment of a global economy, relying solely on precedent is costly, both in terms of dollars and in a company's ability to foster the skill to unlearn and relearn among its employees.

"Yes and" – Improvisation's Golden Rule

Improvisation depends on the golden rule of "Yes and." In improvisation, we agree to accept ideas (sometimes referred to as "offers") from others without judging ("yes") and to build upon those ideas ("and") to see where they take us.

I want to make something perfectly clear here. *Accepting* ideas from others doesn't mean that we necessarily *agree* with those ideas. It simply means that we agree to explore the idea to see where it takes us. One of the first lessons I learned as a comedy writer is that any idea is better than no idea. An idea gives us a place to start building a story. The story may take some crazy twists and turns – the story may end up not working. But it gives us a jumping off place to explore. The final script may have nothing to do with the original idea, but by agreeing to explore the idea and add to it, we can end up with something wonderful and rich.

> *"The concept of yes and…is the foundation for building effective teams."*

In business, improv games like "Sell This" (page 128) and "Innovate or Die" (page 131) offer concrete examples of how saying "yes and" can lead to discovery. Saying yes to an idea doesn't commit an individual, team or company to bringing the idea to fruition. It does, however, commit the individual, team or company to exploring the possibilities of the idea. And it's often in this exploration of one idea that we come up with others.

Through improvisation, we can get to the point where it's easy to come up with a dozen reasons why an idea <u>will</u> work. And in today's business climate, we *want* to live in the land of "why this idea will work." The alternative is too painful…and unproductive.

The Land of No

What if you went to work every day, knowing that none of your ideas would be judged negatively? What if you were confident that your co-workers and leaders would try to contribute to your ideas to make them work? You'd look forward to sharing, wouldn't you? You'd stop withholding, right?

Unfortunately, right now, too many people still live in the land of "no" and the land of "no" is bad for business. A stark case in point is that of the two Steves – Jobs and Wosniak – and a little gizmo they built together called the personal computer. According to Jobs, they went to Atari and said, "Hey, we've got this amazing thing, even built with some of your parts, and what do you think about funding us? Or we'll give it to you. We just want to do it. Pay our salary; we'll come work for you. And they (Atari) said no. So then we went to Hewlett-Packard and they said, 'Hey, we don't need you. You haven't gotten through college yet.'"[19] So the two Steves went on to do their own thing. They founded Apple and the rest, as they say, is history.

Or what about Chester Carlson? He invented xerography is 1938. He offered the technology to virtually every major office equipment company in this country. They all said no. He refused to give up on his invention. His wife grew frustrated and divorced him. Bad move on her part – Carlson eventually made more than 150 million bucks from his invention and his original xerox copier is now in the Smithsonian.

And then there's Fred Smith, who came up with the idea for Fed Ex while he was still a student at Yale. The U.S. Postal Service, UPS – even his business professor at the time – all gave the idea a thumbs down. Said it would never work, that no one would pay a premium price for speedy and reliable delivery. Fed Ex launched in 1973 with the delivery of 7 packages. Today, Fed Ex has the largest share of the air express market in the world.

Countless other examples exist.

Think of the last time you were in a team meeting or brainstorming session and you pitched out an idea and the person in charge said "No." Did you withhold further ideas because you were afraid they'd get shot down, too? What ultimately happens to team cohesion and a team's desire to pursue a goal when their ideas are constantly shot down? What happens to morale? To engagement?

If the land of "no" is so detrimental to business, why do we keep saying it?

Why We Say "No"

- Unfortunately, just like in Hollywood, saying "no" can become a habit. "We've always done it this way." Pretty soon, it's a lot easier to come up with a dozen reasons why something won't work than it is to come up with one reason why it will.

- We can be too quick to say "no" when an idea appears unworkable. The idea of people paying more money to have stuff delivered might seem unworkable at first blush, but if we agree to accept a premise unconditionally (without judgment) and explore where it takes us, we can discover that the idea has merit after all. And even if we eventually conclude that an idea is unworkable, we may discover other ideas during that exploration that <u>are</u> workable.

- It's often easier to say "no". Saying "yes" requires action. When we say "yes" to an idea we have to expend energy to pursue it.

- Sometimes we say "no" because we don't like the person who came up with the idea.

- Sometimes we say "no" simply because we have an idea of our own that we like better.

- Some leaders say "no" because they believe they should be the ones who have all the ideas. They're more concerned with idea geography (where did the idea come from?) than in idea generation. That's a dangerous position for a leader to take. Employees whose ideas are continually ignored will become frustrated and move on – maybe to the competition. As I mentioned earlier, the lines between management and worker in the Knowledge Era have blurred almost to the point of being non-existent when it comes to knowledge. Companies have to draw on the knowledge of all their workers. Restricting idea generation to those in a leadership role undercuts a company's ability to stay competitive.

- Sometimes it's a "hairball". Gordon MacKenzie, a writer and creative director for Hallmark cards for 30 years, wrote a book entitled "Orbiting the Giant Hairball." The hairball he refers to is the collection of often counterproductive rules, policies and procedures that seem to exist in some companies that make it difficult for innovative ideas to see the light of day.[20] Are you orbiting a hairball where you work? If you do things a certain way simply because they've always been done that way…you're saying no.

So…how do we break out of the land of "no" and move into the neighborhood of "why this idea will work"?

Simple. By embracing improvisation's golden rule of "yes and."

The Power of "Yes and"

Remember, in improvisation we agree to accept all ideas from others without judging and to build on those ideas to see where they take us.

The concept of "yes and" in improvisation is the foundation for building effective teams, enhancing the skills needed for collaboration. We humans first needed to work together – foraging for food, fending off predators – to ensure our very survival. We now need to work together to ensure our survival in today's global marketplace.

> *"Restricting idea generation to those in a leadership role undercuts a company's ability to stay competitive."*

Effective Teams Ensure Business Success

In study after study of organizational effectiveness, the single dimension that mattered most was the human element and how workers interacted with one another in teams. As John Seely Brown, former director of the Xerox Palo Alto Research Center, puts it: "Everything is done collaboratively. There are no lone geniuses anywhere. We traffic in human capital; ideas don't come from a lone head, but from collaboration in a deep sense."[21]

Improvisation, through a simple game like "Yes And" (page 134) helps us connect with our fellow workers, building bonds that lead to collaboration. That collaboration leads to consilience – the unity of all knowledge.

It's "Yes and" - Not "Yes but"

In using the concept of "Yes and" it's important to listen for the concept of "no." People new to the practice of improvisation sometimes don't recognize that they're saying "yes but."

For example, in one improv exercise, "Innovate or Die" (page 131), teams try to come up with new ways to use an everyday product, like paperclips. During a recent workshop, one team member suggested making chain mail from them. Another team member said, "Okay, but nobody wears chain mail anymore." And another said, "Okay, but we'll have to retool to accommodate welding them together." Neither team member recognized that they were, in effect, shooting down the idea of chain mail by adding a caveat.

It's important to remind the team that the golden rule is "Yes and" – not "Yes but." If participants fall into "Yes but," it's good to stop the improv and ask the team how they might have expressed their thoughts differently. Sometimes, it only takes rephrasing the sentence: "Okay and we'll retool so we can weld them." Other times, the roadblock goes beyond the word "but". The idea that no one wears chain mail any longer effectively shuts down the creative process.

More Subtle Roadblocks

Sometimes a roadblock can be even more subtle. People say "no" in non-verbal ways as well. They may embrace a game with little enthusiasm or their body language may be closed when others are offering ideas, which sends a negative message. They may simply refuse to play at all.

You can't force someone to take part in improvisation. But experience has shown me that if you continue to provide positive feedback to the players who engage in a game, they'll not only have fun – they'll also reach a positive outcome.

More than anything else, watching their co-workers have a good time and connect with one another will influence those who are reluctant to "play" to join in.

"Very few people would listen if they didn't know it was their turn to speak next."[22]
Robert Conklin, Educator

"There are people who, instead of listening to what is being said to them, are already listening to what they are going to say themselves."[23]
Albert Guinon, Writer

Chapter Seven
Listening – The Bedrock of Communication

According to my parents, I started talking in full sentences before I was two. Apparently I was one of those kids who never shut up. Nothing got by me without a question or a comment. Both my parents worked full time so child rearing duties fell to my grandmother, who'd raised 5 kids on her own after being widowed. You'd think one more wouldn't faze her, but apparently my constant chatter tried even her patience and one day she turned to me, exasperated, "Why do you think God gave you two ears and one mouth?!"

At the time I thought it was because we'd look pretty silly if it was the other way around. But it was my grandmother's way of saying that if people listened twice as much as they spoke, the world would be a better place. I think she was right - as long as we're listening effectively.

According to linguists, we spend up to 80% of our waking hours in some form of communication: writing (9%), reading (16%), speaking (30%) or listening (45%).[24] As you can see, the biggest part of this communication is listening. It's the bedrock of communication because it's by listening that we share knowledge. And by sharing knowledge, we create the all-important knowledge groups so vital to success in business today.

What Do You Know?

There's a saying in today's workplace – no one can know everything. Robert Kelley, of Carnegie-Mellon University, has been asking people working at a number of companies the same question every year: "What percentage of the knowledge that you need to do your job is stored in your own mind?" In 1986, the answer was about 75%. By 1997, the percentage had slipped to between 15-20% and by 2006, it was down to 8-10%. No doubt that this percentage has slipped even lower today. [25]

On top of the above, the amount of knowledge in the world has doubled over the last decade. It's no wonder that we all feel overwhelmed at the amount of info coming our way every day.

And even once we know something, we can't count on it to stay relevant. There's a concept called the half-life of knowledge. It's a concept attributed to the economist Fritz Machlup. Half-life simply refers to the time span between when knowledge is gained and when it becomes obsolete. Today, on average, knowledge reaches obsolescence in 500 days…but can be much quicker in some areas.[26] That means we have to keep learning more just to stay afloat.

Staggering, isn't it?

The "Group Mind"

Because of this knowledge explosion, most companies have turned to the concept of teams and collaboration to take advantage of what Daniel Goleman refers to as "the group mind." Others refer to it as a knowledge group. No matter what you call it, this knowledge group is our network or team of people we have available to us as resources to provide information and expertise.

Since no one of us can know everything – and we know from research that teams often outperform individuals – it makes sense to take advantage of this knowledge group. But we can't take advantage of it without effective communication. That's vital to the success of group dynamics. And effective communication starts with effective listening.

How We Listen

I'd like to think becoming an effective listener is as easy as just paying more attention to the people we communicate with. An exercise like "The Awareness Quiz" (page 140) proves that it's not. The truth is that most of us have developed some bad habits when it comes to listening and those habits have to be broken.

Think about the last conversation you had. What was going through your mind as the other person was speaking? If we're honest, we may have to admit that there were two conversations going on - the actual one and the tape that's running in our heads, where we map out how we want the conversation to go and what we're going to say to keep it on track. We're listening to the other person just enough so that we'll know when it's our turn to jump back into the conversation. We call this "listening to reply."

We've seen examples of the "listen to reply" style hundreds of times during political press conferences. A member of the press asks a question and the politician answers the question he or she had intended to answer all along. If the politician's really good, we may not notice that's what happened. Other times, the answer given has no relation at all to the question that was asked.

When we "listen to reply" we focus more on ourselves and less on the other person, which means that we often fail to pick up on non-verbal cues. Non-verbal cues can often help us determine the intent of what someone is saying. Non-verbal cues may prod us to dig deeper for more information if we sense that the person we're speaking to is holding back, perhaps unintentionally. (More about non-verbal cues later.)

Listen to Understand

To be an effective listener, we have to "listen to understand." Our goal is to take in information without any pre-conceived ideas and to respond to that information effectively "in the moment". In order to move forward, either as individuals or in teams, we have to be able to assess information and then decide what to do about it. It's impossible to assess information if we haven't heard it. And we won't *hear* it if we're too focused on getting our own ideas out there at the expense of listening to what others have to say.

Awareness Listening

Think of a time when you found yourself in conversation with someone and you "drifted off." You know what I mean. One moment you're hearing what they're saying and then a moment later you realize you haven't heard the last few words they've said and you're lost. What happened?

People speak 100-175 words per minute (WPM). We can listen intelligently to 600-800 WPM. That means our brain isn't fully engaged and a brain that's not fully engaged is a restless brain. A restless brain seeks out something else to engage it. And all too often, that something else is our own thoughts.

But when we "listen to understand," our restless brains *are* doing something else. We're aware of much more than the words we exchange. We make note of our physical surroundings and the way we feel during a conversation. We make note of eye contact, gestures and body language. We observe these things and then draw inferences from those observations.

I remember a session of "The Awareness Quiz" with a group of co-workers from a brokerage. During the debrief, I asked each participant to share one inference they drew from their observation/conversation.

One woman said she suggested she and her partner take part in the exercise sitting down because she noticed that her partner was wearing flats, something she said her co-worker would never do unless she had an injury of some kind. It turns out that her co-worker had indeed turned her ankle ice skating the previous week-end. The co-worker said that while she didn't share the info with her partner, she appreciated being seated and thought her increased comfort helped her concentrate more effectively.

Listening for Intent

Like the example above, we all want to draw the correct inferences when we engage in communicating with others. And we do that by listening for intent. What's the point the other person is trying to make? What's the most important part of the message? What's its emotional content? Intent is more difficult to identify than you think.

> *"When we listen to understand and discover intent, we create an arena for collaboration."*

A very good friend of mine from my early years in theatre fell madly in love with a fellow actor. Unfortunately for her, when they first met he was already involved with another woman who would become his wife. But my friend never got over him – she never married and carried a torch for him for years.

It was some years later when my friend and I unexpectedly ran into this fellow. We all went for coffee, where he confided that he'd had a very rough year. Since he and his wife had divorced several years ago, he'd been living on the East Coast, where he and his twin brother had opened a restaurant together. His brother had recently been killed in an auto accident and he couldn't keep the restaurant going on his own. The first thing out of my friend's mouth was, "You and Wendy divorced?"

Now, I think we can all agree that my friend did a poor job of assessing the information that we were given. The fact that this man had been divorced years earlier was peripheral information to the main story. It was simply a way of explaining how he ended up on the East Coast. The primary offer during our exchange was the fact that his twin brother, with whom he had always been close, had been killed.

Think back on a time when your assessment of the information coming at you was flawed. What challenges/problems did that create? And what could you have done differently/better?

The Perfect Arena for Listening

We need to remind ourselves as we listen that it's our responsibility not only to take in information, but then to decide how to prioritize it, correctly interpret it and then frame our responses accordingly. And we have to be careful that when we listen (and send messages for that matter), we don't simply do it through our own filters. In my friend's case, she was still carrying the torch for this guy after all these years. And in her mind, the fact that he was now divorced was the most important information he relayed…because she was listening through her own personal filter. We all have personal filters (our experiences, beliefs, values and attitudes) and we have to be mindful of them, so we can adjust them (which is possible) and reduce the chances of misunderstanding.

Improvisation provides the perfect arena for honing our ability to be effective listeners. Improvisation forces us to "stay in the moment", so that we have to take in facts as they're presented to us. And we exercise our ability to "listen to understand" because listening is the very foundation of improvisation. How we respond during an improv game is completely dependent upon the "offers" we get from others. And because we know that, we're extra vigilant about paying attention and trying to understand our fellow player's intent.

When we "listen to understand" and discover intent, we create an arena for collaboration. Participants know that what they offer will be accepted (and therefore valued). Participants who feel valued contribute more to the group and try hard to communicate their intent, building clarity. And a group's success depends on the contributions of <u>all</u> members. In fact, a team that operates with the full contribution of all its members is destined for success.

A note here – while it's key that we be effective listeners, we also have to take responsibility that we're effective messengers as well. It's not kosher to leave it up to our listeners to ferret out our intent.

Status

I promised more about non-verbal communication later – so here it is. You've heard the saying, "One picture is worth a thousand words." That should tell you something about the power of non-verbal cues when we're communicating. How someone looks, how they stand, how they gesture, what emotions we read on their faces – all of these help us "listen" to their message…*when* we interpret these cues correctly.

We can't discuss non-verbal cues without mentioning status. The most comprehensive explanation of status I've ever come across is in Keith Johnstone's book "Impro: Improvisation and the Theatre".

In fact, he devotes over 40 pages to its discussion and goes into way more detail that we need here. For our purposes a general understanding of status is sufficient. When we speak about status, we're talking about a formal expression of rank.

We all operate in the world, embracing a different status depending upon the situation in which we find ourselves. We behave differently with our peers at work than we do with our superiors. For example, if you're presenting a report to team members, it wouldn't be unusual to go and sit with them at a table as you go over the report. But if you're giving a presentation to your Board of Directors, chances are you won't be "invading their space" by sitting with them to give your presentation.

When we think of status, we also assume that someone's status is higher than ours if their rank is higher, though this isn't always the case. When I first moved to southern California, I took temp jobs as I got myself established. One assignment found me serving as the assistant to a very powerful A&R guy at Warner Brothers records. You had to get past me to get to him so even though I was "only" a temporary assistant, my perceived status was much higher than others in the company whose title was more important than mine.

When It Comes to Status, Let's All Be Equal

So what does all of this have to do with communication? A lot - as it turns out – because each of us decides what status to offer others and what status we'll accept from others. And how people perceive this status and how we perceive the status of others impacts communication. In David Rock's SCARF, a brain-based model for collaborating with and influencing others, he looks at status, the different values people place on status and how we can use it to minimize threats and maximize rewards. It's surprisingly easy to accidentally threaten someone's sense of status simply by giving advice or suggesting that someone might not be up to the task at hand.

> *"What we're talking about here is social dynamics."*

Conversely, we can make people feel better about themselves (and thus increase their status) by offering them opportunities to learn and develop.[27]

Think about this – if, as a leader, you set your status too far above your team members, you increase the barriers between you. Barriers mean less trust. Less trust means that team members are reluctant to engage, to share their ideas. And if they won't share ideas, we can't take advantage of group knowledge.

What we're really talking about here is social dynamics – how do we relate to one another and how does that affect our ability to communicate? An improve exercise like "Pecking Order" (page 165) gives participants an opportunity to explore the concept of status and how it can impact our day to day interactions.

We can add another layer to social dynamics when we consider that today's work environment often has four separate generations working side by side (soon to be joined by a fifth, sometimes referred to as linksters). Bringing multiple generations together can sometimes result in inter-generational conflict, with each generation forming a sometimes hasty and wrong impression of other generations. And when it comes to status, each generation brings its own idea of where it (and other generations) belongs. For example, both Traditionalists and Boomers tend to see themselves "above" Gen Xers and Millenials, simply by virtue of experience.

It's important that all of us are aware of status. When we're able to equalize status, it helps generate and maintain the free flow of knowledge. If members of a team feel equal to one another, it's more likely that everyone will participate. And as we said, a successful team depends on every one of its members. You'll find games in the back of this book you can use to explore the concept of status. The ability to influence it can be powerful.

"The organizations of the future will increasingly depend on the creativity of its members to survive."
Warren Bennis[28]

Chapter Eight

Creativity

"Creativity requires the courage to let go of certainties."
Erich Fromm[29]

"Creativity involves breaking out of established patterns to look at things in a different way."
Edward deBono[30]

"To be successful, we must live from our imaginations, not from our memories."
Steven Covey[31]

Ramp Up Your Creative Mojo

When 940 senior executives from around the world were asked by Boston Consulting Group, Inc. about the importance of creativity to business success, all of them responded that increasing revenues through innovation was essential to their company's success.[32] Major corporations like Procter & Gamble and General Electric Co. are already harnessing the new core competency – creativity – to generate top-line growth. To compete in today's global economy, all companies are going to have to ramp up their creative mojo. Leaders and team members may not find that so easy, given the things that get in the way of our being creative.

"Functional Fixedness"

One obstacle to being creative is that we rely on things that have worked in the past. Psychologists call it "functional fixedness." Being creative means we have to break down old patterns and stop doing things the same way we've always done them. Too often, industry leaders fail to come up with the next iteration because they're perfectly happy with things as they are and fail to see the need to innovate.

> *"To compete in today's global economy, all companies are going to have to ramp up their creative mojo."*

Remember the story about Schwinn? The company tried to rely on designs that had worked for them in the past, and that reliance drove them into bankruptcy.

In the early 1960's, one of Republic Steel's key customers – the canning industry – turned to aluminum. Republic's CEO at the time called aluminum the "weak metal" and vowed never to give up on steel.[33] The company's now kaput.

An internal memo from Western Union said of the telephone: "It has too many shortcomings to be seriously considered as a means of communication. The device is inherently of no value to us."[34] When's the last time you got a telegram?

Montgomery Ward was displaced by other retailers because it failed to keep its image current and neglected to expand when it had the chance.[35]

And love it or hate it, fifteen years ago Microsoft had the edge in technology. In the last decade, however, Apple created the iPod, the iPhone, the iPad, the iCloud and the iTunes store. Google dominates Internet search, Amazon dominates online retail, launched a business that rents out computer power and data storage and is looking to make deliveries via drones. Microsoft now finds itself trying to catch up.

It's not surprising that organizations and leaders continue to rely on doing business the way they've always done it. It's scary to let go of the familiar and embrace the unknown. But if we're unwilling to innovate, we can kiss our ability to be competitive goodbye.

Criticism Kills

The biggest killer of creativity is criticism. I once read that Sir Isaac Newton was so sensitive to criticism that he withheld the publication of a paper on optics for 15 years until his chief critic died, thereby delaying the introduction of his reflecting telescope. We all know that it takes courage to "stick our necks out" and if our efforts are met with criticism, it'll be harder to speak up the next time.

During my writing career, I spent a lot of time in writers' rooms. The writers' room is where all the writers gather to pitch ideas, beat out stories and do group rewrites on scripts. The ideal writers' room is sacrosanct – like Vegas, what happens in the writers' room stays in the writers' room. A productive writers' room is a free-wheeling one, where anyone says anything, knowing that if one joke or story point doesn't stick to the wall, it might inspire someone else to deliver.

The unwritten rule is – don't pass judgment. Most of us know not every joke we pitch is drop dead funny. But knowing that nobody's going to shoot you down for a joke that bombs is what gives writers the courage to keep pitching.

One of the best writers' rooms I ever experienced was run by Chuck Lorre (the creator of such shows as "Grace Under Fire," "Dharma and Greg," "Two and a Half Men," "Mike & Molly," "The Big Bang Theory" and "Mom"). Chuck taught me more about comedy than almost anyone I worked with. And his writers' room was the best – encouraging, collaborative, fearless (unless you were watching the clock, wondering when you'd get to go home). I did some of my best work with him.

Another writer who is aces to work with is Russ Woody. (His credits include "Cybill," for which he won a Golden Globe, "Hill Street Blues," "Newhart," "Murphy Brown," for which he won an Emmy, "The Middle" and many others.) I never heard Russ say "no" to an idea anyone pitched – it was always "maybe," which kept the door open for all of us.

I've worked with great stand ups like Jeff Foxworthy and Ritch Shydner. I'm no stand up. It could have been intimidating pitching jokes alongside those guys. It wasn't…because they were both open and generous and encouraging and non-judgmental which gave me the courage to keep pitching. And I know my work was better for having worked with them.

> *"The biggest killer of creativity is criticism."*

I've also had the misfortune of the opposite experience. During a staff job early in my career, I found myself on a show where the writers' room was a nightmare. We all censored ourselves, trying to pitch the perfect joke, knowing the executive producer was just waiting to nail us if the joke fell short. One incident in particular stands out.

A funny and genuinely nice guy on the staff pitched a joke (which the rest of us thought was darn good) and the head honcho ridiculed him. The chastised writer tried to make a joke out of it but from that day forward, the staff shut down. All our energy was spent second guessing ourselves. Because none of us wanted to be humiliated, spontaneity died and creativity was choked off. The series barely limped along for two seasons and I would venture to say that no one (save the creator) thought she or he did their best work under those circumstances.

As a leader, you have to ask yourself how your behavior impacts creativity in your organization. Do you provide a work climate where employees are free to think out loud without judgment? Are they encouraged to take risks and possibly fail? Are they confident that failure won't be met with recrimination? Do your employees know that their contributions are valued? Is there a free and open exchange of ideas? Have you created a work climate that encourages and supports collaboration?

Have you created a place to thrive?

Oh Spontaneity, Where Art Thou?

You can't mention creativity without shining a spotlight on spontaneity. Many consider spontaneity to be the bedrock of creativity, that without it, creativity wouldn't exist. I am one of those folks.

Spontaneity is a moment of self-expression, free from thought and free from judgment. It's a natural impulse – we act without effort or premeditation. We rely on instinct alone and react to something in the moment.

While most of us might embrace the concept of spontaneity, it eludes us in practice. Improv games like "Pass the Frog" (page 86), "Sound Circle" (page 92) and "Barney" (page 95) help us learn to trust our instincts and be comfortable reacting "in the moment."

We want to keep spontaneity alive to allow for the full flower of creative expression. If we're facilitating an improv game, that means keeping the room "safe" – encouraging people to trust their instincts, providing positive feedback on their efforts and, above all, making sure that others don't pass judgment on the "offers."

Our Inner Critic

Unfortunately for most of us, we are our own worst critic. We often judge our own ideas and thoughts harshly ("That's a dumb idea, why did I offer it?" or "I can't believe I said something so stupid. It can't possibly work."). Michael Ray, the Stanford Business School Professor who created classes on creativity, dubbed it "the voice of judgment."[36] In improvisation, we refer to that voice as our "inner critic." It's our "inner critic" that so often keeps us from being spontaneous, which prevents us from retrieving our own creativity.

That same "inner critic" also prevents us from going outside boundaries to find alternative solutions to problems. It stops us from looking at challenges in new ways…and that kind of censorship comes at a premium.

Does Creativity = Genius?

By the time they're adults, most people think it requires some kind of genius to be creative or that there's a certain "creative type". But the fact is, almost all of the research done on creativity shows that anyone with normal intelligence is capable of being creative. Surprised?

Think back to when you were a kid. I'll bet you could spend hours "acting out" stories from your imagination. We all took common objects like pots and pans and turned them into musical instruments or made cardboard boxes into castles. We built forts out of snow or old blankets and sticks and beat back our "enemies" with icy ammunition or dried mud balls. And didn't we, in the simple act of playing dress up, become someone else? I don't know many of us who would consider ourselves a genius as a child and yet we were certainly creative. Even kids today, who can spend so much time playing video games, still make up incredibly imaginative home lives for the characters in these games.

Creativity – Where Art Thou?

So what happened to all that creativity?

Research done by Psychologist and Harvard Business School Professor Teresa Amabile answers that question by identifying what she calls the 5 killers of creativity that help destroy that instinctual creative side we have as children.[37]

- Surveillance – hovering over kids, making them feel like they're constantly being watched.

- Evaluation – making kids worry about how others judge what they do.

- Competition – putting kids in win/lose situations, where only one kid can come out on top.

- Over control – telling kids exactly how to do something.

- Pressure – establishing expectations that are out of a child's reach.

When I look at these criteria, I remember one specific instance in my life when they were all at play…and it changed me for a long time. I was in kindergarten and we were coloring a picture of a turkey.

- My teacher walked the aisles, looking over our shoulders to see how our drawings were coming along. (surveillance)

- When she stopped at my desk, she took my drawing, held it up for the class and said, "Turkeys don't have blue feathers." (evaluation)

- "Did anyone else make their turkey's feathers the wrong color?" (competition – who else "loses"?)

- Then the teacher took away all my crayons except for the brown, black and white ones and told me to finish my feathers using the "right" colors. (over control)

- And she admonished me to stay inside the lines. (pressure)

Up until that day, I was in love with color and would draw with abandon. After that experience, I censored how I colored, asking myself if I was using the "right" colors and whether the other kids would think my drawings were "wrong."

> *"Improvisation offers a concrete way to retrieve and grow your creativity."*

By the time we're adults in the workplace, we've had enough of these kinds of experiences to choke off creativity many times over. At one time or another, we've all been micromanaged. Routine performance reviews can seem more like excuses to judge than opportunities for development. With companies determined to do more with less, we're often asked to achieve goals in spite of lacking necessary resources. And some leaders still insist that pitting employees against one another is the best way to "win."

But without creativity, there is no "win." And getting creativity back means learning to trust our instincts again, embrace spontaneity and react in the moment. That takes practice. But it's something all of us can do – and must do – in order to reclaim our ability to transcend habitual ways of thinking and doing.

You CAN Retrieve Your Creativity

Improvisation offers a concrete way to retrieve and grow your creativity.

For starters, improvisation is fun. And humor greases the wheels of creativity. Having fun helps disarm your inner critic. Through studying and practicing improvisation as an actor, I learned to "go with my gut," to follow my impulses, which is the foundation for creating. Since improvisation takes place "in the moment," our actions during the exercises come from impulse.

As participants in improvisation, we agree not to judge. Any idea offered is a valid idea and one on which we can build. There is no "right" or "wrong" in improvisation so we don't have to fear being judged by others.

In improvisation, we work within a framework in which all of the participants work together toward a successful outcome. We depend upon one another – when one of us succeeds in building on a previous offer, we all succeed. It's a win/win for everyone in the "game."

The more we practice improvisation, the more self-confident we become in embracing our impulses. Once we're able to more freely embrace those impulses, our creativity blossoms and we no longer feel the necessity to hang on to old patterns.

Something to Think About….

Pierre Omidyar's wife collected Pez dispensers. She was having a hard time building her collection through traditional ways. Pierre thought about his wife's predicament and came to the conclusion that what she needed was a new and different way to get in touch with people who had dispensers to sell. What about an online garage sale?[38]

Pierre's online garage sale became e-Bay. And he became a billionaire…because he dared to "get outside the box" and think creatively. And So….

If you're ready to challenge your habitual ways of thinking and doing…
If you're up for a risk…
If you want to be able to move forward in the face of ambiguity…
If you're ready to build more collaborative teams…
If you want others to perceive you as someone who really listens…
If you're eager to reclaim your creativity…

Then turn the page….and let the games begin.

Chapter Nine

Before We Begin

I know. I know. I said turn the page and let the games begin. And they will. I just have a few final thoughts.

Setting the Stage – Where the Heck are We Going to Do This?

We can practice improvisation anywhere, as long as there's enough space to spread out and move around comfortably. I prefer going "off-site" if I'm working with folks all from the same company. It helps to get people away from their usual workplace distractions and by changing their environment we begin the first step in changing habitual ways of thinking and doing. If you find yourself having to facilitate on site, make sure you see the venue and have time to change it/add to it before you meet with your group.

Privacy Please

Chances are most people won't have much experience with improvisation. And when you mention improvisation to people in business, their first response might be "I'm not funny" or "I don't want to be in the spotlight." Remind the group that successful improvisers don't try to be funny. Funny is what happens when we have honest discovery and reaction to everyday life. Acknowledge that people have different levels of comfort when it comes to being "the center of attention." Many of the games are made for small groups so people don't have to feel like everyone's watching them.

When we practice these games with a group that works together, we're also asking these people to get outside their normal working relationships with colleagues. Most of us show certain parts of ourselves to the people we work with. Improvisation asks us to go outside those parameters, which can be intimidating.

In order to counter these feelings and help participants embrace improvisation, it's up to you to provide a safe environment. Above all, the venue should be private.

Windows that open onto public walkways and allow people passing by to "peek in" to see what's going on can make people feel self-conscious. And nothing dampens the creative spirit more than having someone poke their head in and ask the group to "quiet down." The room should have enough sound proofing so that people don't worry about being too loud.

Set the Mood

Improvisation is fun. Improvisation is freeing. What people do is influenced by their environment, so set the mood. I often take a life-sized soft sculpture named Pat with me to workshops. She sits in a chair holding a big sign that says, "Yes and" as a reminder of improvisation's golden rule. She also helps when it comes to the HOV lanes. Unfortunately, she doesn't fly well as she's too big to carry on and frankly, I'm too cheap to buy her a seat. (If I know Pat as well as I think I do, she'd insist on a seat in first class.)

Have bunches of colorful balloons tied around the room. Use pillows instead of chairs. Put out plenty of snacks in colorful bowls. Let your own creativity reign to take your space as far away as you can from the standard "meeting room." If there's a private space outdoors, consider moving your group there for at least part of the workshop.

Tick Tock

No clocks in the room. Don't be a slave to father time. Don't sweat it if you don't get through as many games as you wanted to. It's more important to let the games play out, to see where the group takes them.

And don't skimp on the debrief because you feel pressed for time. People need to know that what they've experienced can be used to be more effective in their day-to-day work lives. People need to know that time spent building the skill to improvise isn't time wasted.

A Note about Adult Learning

If you ask a group of people why adults can't learn, many try to answer the question without challenging its premise.

Adults can learn, they do learn. But they have different requirements as learners and we need to keep that in mind, especially when we ask them to take part in improvisation, which seems so far outside the norm of what we consider an "adult learning experience."

The truth is that most of us like the familiar and are uncomfortable with change. It's lucky for us that our brains like novelty and rush to build new neural pathways whenever we're exposed to something new. But that doesn't mean there won't be barriers.

Anxiety is the Enemy

Although improvisation is gaining credibility in business, it's still a new process to most people. And because they don't fully understand how it works and have no experience with it, anxiety builds when they think about doing it. "Will I fail?" "Will I look foolish in front of my co-workers?" Anxiety drives learning down so, as a facilitator, you need to manage that anxiety.

One way we manage the anxiety is simply to acknowledge it. Identify the elephant in the room and concede that most people are nervous when they first try improvisation. That's why warm up games are so important.

Don't skip the warm ups, even if you're pressed for time.

Warm up games invite participants to "get out of their heads" and be present in the moment. A warm up game is a first opportunity for players to let go of control and be open to what's happening around them.

What's the Point?

To the degree that we live in a world of constant change, we need to continue to learn throughout our lives. But adults are <u>motivated</u> to learn in very specific ways:

- Adults will commit to a learning experience if they understand the goals of the experience and how the experience services those goals.

- Adults will commit to a learning experience if they see a reason for learning (i.e., they must cope with a work-related change). Learning is a means to an end.

- Adults will commit to a learning experience if what they learn is practical in their day to day work life. "How is this relevant to me?"

It's important to remind the group how the practice of improvisation can build skills in many different areas.

Making Mistakes

When adults make mistakes, they tend to take it personally, which affects their self-esteem and self-confidence, which affects their ability to be spontaneous. Remind them often that there is no "right" or "wrong" in improvisation.

Feedback

Adults need feedback. Don't skip the debrief questions. Encourage discussion during the debrief and feel free to come up with questions of your own to add to the session. Adults are active participants in a learning experience and you need to involve them in dialogue about what they did or did not experience during the games.

A Note to Facilitators

Believe. I repeat. Believe. As a facilitator, you must believe in the value of using improvisation as a framework for challenging habitual ways of thinking and doing in order for it to be effective. You're apt to be faced with initial skepticism on the part of many people and organizations. In spite of the fact that improvisation is now taught in many of this country's top business schools and is being introduced in top medical schools, not everyone in the work arena will be ready to jump on board.

I'm confident that practicing improvisation and honing the skills one uses to play these games will help make you more comfortable in taking a risk and speaking up. You'll be less stressed by ambiguity and able to move forward in spite of it. Practicing improvisation can help you rediscover your creativity and make you a more effective listener and communicator. Committing to the practice of improvisation will strengthen your ability to collaborate and make you a sought after team member. And all of these skills will add to your organization's effectiveness. I've seen it happen.

A Glossary of Improv Terms

The following is a list of terms used in teaching and practicing improvisation. It helps to be familiar with these terms and to give a copy to participants. Again, sharing a common language helps participants understand more clearly what they're being asked to do.

Accepting – Embracing the offers made by other performers in order to advance the scene.

Advancing – The process of moving the scene forward.

Blocking – Rejecting information or ideas offered by another player. This is one of the most common problems experienced by new improvisers.

Driving – Taking over a scene and not letting other performers influence its direction.

Gibberish* – A nonsense language. (In using gibberish, I've found it much easier to give players a nonsense language [say using the word "blah, blah, blah" or "yada, yada, yada" over and over] rather than have them come up with a nonsense language of their own. Inexperienced improvisers can get focused on creating the language and lose the sense of the point of concentration.)

Narrative – The story told by a scene. Scenes should have a clear beginning, middle and end.

Offer – Any dialog or action which advances the scene. Offers should always be accepted. ("Yes and" concept.)

Point of Concentration – What the scene is about or the task to be completed.

Platform – The who, what and where of a scene. The success of a scene often depends upon having a solid platform.

Status – A character's sense of self-worth. Many scenes are built around status transfers, in which one character's status drops while another's rises. Physical environments and objects also have status.

Transformation – Turning something into something else (one character into another, one object into another, one environment into another).

Yes And – Improvisation's golden rule. As improvisers, we accept our partner's offer and agree to build on it.

The 5 Stages of Improvisation

Don't be surprised if there are those who don't take to improvisation right away. Don't get discouraged. You can keep the group (and yourself) moving forward as long as you know what to expect. That's why I'm sharing "The 5 Stages of Improvisation" with you.

- **Resistance** - It's common for people to resist improvisation at first. Improv asks you to take a risk and put yourself out there and wing it. But improvisation is like playing any sport – the more you play, the better you become.

- **Acceptance** – People are likely to reach this stage more quickly with effective warm-up games. These games are simple and get creative juices flowing. They also give the group a taste of how much fun improv can be.

- **Challenge** - As you move the group into more complex games, players are challenged to push the creative envelope, to go outside habitual ways of interacting and discover insights they wouldn't normally access in everyday life.

- **Frustration** – It's not unusual for some people to become frustrated if they think they're not succeeding at the games. This frustration can rear its head in different ways. Some players may disengage. Some may become angry. Some may question why they're even doing improvisation. Encourage them to hang on, remind them to focus on their POC (Point of Concentration). I've seen some of the best improv work done when people are on the verge of giving up.

- **Breakthrough** - It's that glorious moment when everything clicks, when players lock on to a new and surprising discovery about themselves…that they CAN "think on their feet."

Okay, now on to the next page…

And let the games begin. For real.

The Games

Introduction

I refer to this section as The Games, simply because most people would consider a game to be fun and improvisation is fun. I also like the word "game" as adverb – "I am game" – which describes to me a person who is bold, courageous and spirited. People who are willing to explore improvisation are all those things and anyone who steps forward to "play" should be recognized as such.

Having said that, some of you may feel that business professionals aren't likely to embrace or will see as frivolous a thing labeled a "game." In that case, you may want to refer to these games as exercises or activities or challenges. Or you can come up with your own appellation which you think best suits your needs. Regardless of what we name what we do, let's never lose sight of the value of improvisation and that it is, in the words of improv expert Izzy Gesell, "a ropes course for the mind."

There are literally hundreds of improv games available and I couldn't begin to include them all. I offer the ones I've found most useful during my own work with individuals, businesses and organizations.

Most of the games included here are available in a variety of resources – I've included a list of resources in the back of this guide. Many of these games are ones I first encountered during my early years in theatre in high school and college, and later with the Eureka Theatre Company of San Francisco. I was introduced to them by a long list of fellow performers, directors, writers, stand up comics and professors, to whom I owe much thanks for having helped awaken my own creative spirit. I hope I've thanked them often during the times we've spent together. If I haven't, please forgive me and know that I appreciate everything I learned from all of you.

Some of these games are known by more than one name – for example, I remember being introduced to "Ask a Silly Question" by a theatre professor at the University of Missouri, but it was known at that time by the less politically correct name of "Ask a Dumb Question."

One of the most exciting things about improvisation is that it's organic – you can play the same game with different people and discover new insights with each group. Take note of these insights – I encourage you to pass them on to others and to use them in your own continued work with business professionals. And as always, improvisation invites you – encourages you – to adapt these games to fit other purposes you uncover.

Format

For each game, I've included a general description of the game and its goals. The beauty of improvisation is that the games go to strengthen a variety of skills, rather than just one, so you'll see more than one goal listed for each game.

I've also indicated what materials or props you'll need for each game, how many participants can "play" and the time it will take to complete the exercise. If the number of participants is 6-10, this means that 6-10 participants can play the game together at the same time. You can always play the game a second – or third – time if you have a larger group. In some cases, I've included variations which give the game a different twist for participants who play the game after its initial introduction. And "time" refers only to the exercise itself and doesn't include the time you'll spend on the debrief.

Depending on the size of your group, not everyone is going to be able to take part in every game. Those who aren't players in a specific game still have an important role to play – that of the "audience." During the explanation of the games, when I refer to "audience", I'm talking about the participants who aren't actively engaged in the game at the moment.

I've also included a series of questions you can feel free to ask during the debrief session, and I'm sure you'll want to come up with your own debrief questions as well. (Note that some of the questions are valid only when you've used the variations of the game that are offered.)

The debrief session is vital. Participants have to be able to make the connection between the game and the skills the game builds and how those skills are relevant and applicable to their everyday work lives.

It's important to involve everybody in the debrief process. In working with a group where some participants are reluctant to participate, I've found it helpful to hand out a list of the debrief questions after the game, break the group into dyads and give them an opportunity to discuss the questions with one another and write down their responses before we explore the questions as a group.

I sometimes use actual work situations as the basis for improvisation, as that makes it easier for the participants to make that connection. Be aware, however, that using real situations encountered at work may produce not an improvisation, but a rehashing of what actually happened. Then as facilitators and coaches, we have to take that experience and rework it with the participants, helping them discover new approaches and new outcomes.

If a game bogs down, simply stop the game, remind participants what the goal(s) of the game are and start over. Or end it and move on to another game with similar goals.

Not every game works with every group or situation. After a debrief of the new game, you might try revisiting the original game and see what outcome occurs this time. Or you may simply move on to another new exercise.

As always, feel free to add to or change the games to suit you – in other words, improvise!

I'd love it if you shared your own experiences with the games and I want to hear your ideas, different approaches, "takes" and questions you add. Just email me at jenniea@doboldwork.com

Warm Ups

Warm up games do more than "warm us up" to improvise but we call them "warm ups" because that's their primary function and they are often simpler in structure than other games and the group catches on to them quickly.

Never skip a warm up, even if a group has worked together before.

Warm ups give us the perfect opportunity to follow our impulses while there's very little at stake. And for groups that haven't worked much or at all together, it gives everyone a chance to find a comfort level with one another. It also gives everyone permission to be silly and sets a lighter tone for the improvisational work to follow.

Warm Up #1
Ask a Silly Question

Description
Ask each member of the group a silly question. Keep in mind that there are no wrong answers, which helps remove the risk of appearing foolish by saying something silly.

Goals
- An ice breaker, to loosen up the group.
- To lose feelings of being self-conscious.
- To experience spontaneity.
- To experience non-judgment.

Number of Participants
Unlimited, but works best when you have at least 6 people.

Time
5-10 minutes, depending upon the number of participants

Materials
None, although it's easier if you have several silly questions in mind before you start. That way, you can focus on the facilitation of the game instead of on coming up with silly questions.

Process
Have everyone stand comfortably in a circle. (I usually start a group standing – I find that people are more energized when they're on their feet than when they're sitting. And being in a circle makes it easier for us to make eye contact with one another. Making eye contact helps break down barriers between people and can speed the loosening up process.)

Introduce the goals of the game.
Tell the group, "I'm going to ask each of you, at random, a

silly question. Answer quickly with the first thing that comes to mind. Don't censor yourself and don't worry about trying to think up something clever.

"There are no wrong answers. Any answer you give is correct."

Don't give participants too long to answer – 2-3 seconds tops.

Sample Questions:
1. How do you get a giraffe to be faithful?
2. What does an elephant wear on a hike?
3. If you could have an extra hand, where would you put it?
4. How do you teach a chicken to play the piano?
5. What does an ear of corn hear?
6. What are the 3 scariest numbers?
7. What makes water wet?
8. What flavor is a pine cone?
9. What did the duck say to the crow while they were jogging?
10. How do you bounce a turkey?
11. Where is distraction and how do you get there if you don't drive?
12. How do you walk a fish?
13. How many calories are in a booger?

Variation
If you have an exceptionally large group, have them form smaller groups of six and ask each other silly questions.

Suggested Questions for Debrief

- What thoughts/feelings came up when I said I'd be asking each of you a silly question?

- How was your response to the question affected by knowing that any answer you gave would be correct?

- How did you censor yourself?

- What value is there in asking silly questions?

- What did you discover when you answered with the first thing that popped into your head?

- What did you learn about censoring yourself that you can relate to your experience at work?

- How would knowing that your ideas/solutions wouldn't be negatively judged change your behavior at work?

Warm Up #2
Pass the Frog

Description
Ask each member of the group to name as many things in a category as they can in the time it takes to pass the frog around the circle.

Goals
- To warm up.
- To experience taking a risk in a non-threatening, non-judgmental environment.
- To enhance spontaneity.

Number of Participants
10-20

Time
15-25 minutes, depending on the number of participants

Materials
I use a small stuffed frog, which supports a lighter tone. You can use anything small that can be easily passed from one person to the next.

Process
Have everyone stand comfortably in a circle.
Introduce the goals of the game.

Ask for a volunteer to start. Hand that person the frog, "Now, I want you to name as many things as you can in the category I'm going to give you."

Sample Categories:

Italian Foods	Sports Teams
Boy Bands	Presidents
Foreign Car	Boys'/Girls' Names
Foods that are Crunchy	TV Comedies
Things that are Sticky	Famous Pairs (i.e. Penn & Teller)
Kinds of Flowers	Birds

Variations

You can use letters of the alphabet (say as many words as you can think of that start with the letter "L").

Ask for only one volunteer; after the initial player takes part in the game, that player chooses the next person to play and gives that person the category.

Have the person naming the categories try doing it a second time, this time with eyes closed. (Not being able to see the frog moving around the circle cuts down on stress.)

Suggested Questions for Debrief

- What were you thinking as you watched the frog make its way around the circle?

- Did participants either speed up or slow down passing the frog? If so, what conclusions might we draw about the importance of collaboration?

- Did closing your eyes make any difference?

- How do you think you did? (Many times, participants don't feel they've done well, even though as the facilitator, you never tell them how many answers would be deemed acceptable. The participant is the one placing judgment on her or his performance, which is a concrete example of the "inner critic".)

- How might judging yourself too harshly impact your behavior at work?

- What were some of your thoughts while you were "it"?

- What were you thinking or feeling when your time was over?

- What were you thinking, what were your feelings as you watched others play the game? (This game allows us to observe how others react to pressure, frustration and deadlines.)

Warm Up #3
Keep It Up!

Description
A game where the group works as a team to keep a ball in the air.

Goals
- To warm up.
- To experience working as a team.
- To experience letting go and accepting from others.
- To experience building on offers from others.
- To build communication.
- To build trust.

Number of Participants
5-15

Time
10-15 minutes

Materials
A soft ball, about the size of a volleyball or a soccer ball. The softer the better, although it should have enough heft to it to be able to keep it aloft. (Beach balls work great. I've tried nerf balls as well – thumbs down!)

Process
Introduce the goals of the game.

Players get in a circle. Hand the ball to one person, "You're going to start us off by tossing the ball into the air. The rest of you in the circle take turns hitting the ball to each other, keeping it from touching the ground for as long as you can. No one can hit the ball more than once in a row."

"Try calling out numbers as you hit the ball – 1, 2, 3! Or call out your name as you hit it - Rachel, Monica, Joey, Ross, Phoebe, Chandler!"

Variations

Players can use this game during a brain storming session. They call out ideas each time they hit the ball.

You can use this game during a review session. Each player shouts out a learning point as they hit the ball.

You can have the players tell a story as they keep the ball in the air – each time they hit the ball, they add a word to the story.

Reminder

Although this game seems simple, it provides an excellent opportunity to see how teams operate. You may see players who "hog" the ball or others who hang back from hitting it. We find these same behaviors in work teams. When one or two members of a team try to control the team, it can intimidate other members who pull back from participation. Effective teams need input from all members.

Suggested Questions for DeBrief

- What helped the group successfully keep the ball in the air?

- Were there any behaviors that hindered the group? In what ways might these behaviors hinder a team at work? What was different when you thought the group was successful as opposed to when you thought it wasn't?

- Were you unwilling to play? Why?

- What were your thoughts or how did you feel when you thought you were responsible for dropping the ball? What parallels can you draw with regard to your participation as part of a work team?

- What did you think when you thought someone else was responsible for dropping the ball? What parallels can you draw with regard to participants on your work team?

- Did you feel support from your fellow team members?

- In what ways were your experiences during this game similar to your experiences with work?

Warm Up #4
Sound Circle

Description
Players pass sounds and gestures to one another, to loosen up physically and vocally.

Goals
- Free physical movement.
- Free vocalizations.
- To lose feelings of self-consciousness.
- To accept from others.
- To experience spontaneity.

Number of Participants
Unlimited.

Time
10-15 minutes, depending on number of participants

Materials
None.

Process
Have everyone stand in a circle, leaving enough space between one another to allow for freedom of movement.

Introduce the goals of the game.

Ask for a volunteer to start the game. "I want you to make a gesture toward the person standing to your right. Pair that gesture with a sound. For example, you might make a gesture as if you're throwing a ball underhanded and pair it with a 'whoosh' sound."

Have the person who "received" the sound and gesture immediately imitate the gesture and sound, then turn to the player on <u>his/her</u> right and make a totally different gesture and sound.

Repeat this same pattern with every participant in the circle.

Encourage players, "Make those gestures big! Experiment with those sounds."

Variations
Have players point to any other player in the circle at random and throw the sound and gesture to them.

Have them play the game as fast as they can.

Suggested Questions for Debrief

- How difficult was it to let go with a big gesture and sound? Why was it difficult?

- How did you censor yourself? How does this kind of censorship show up in your day to day work life?

- What was hardest about this game for you? Can you relate this same difficulty to things you encounter in your work?

- What was easiest about this game for you?

- In what ways was it different when you knew that your turn was coming compared to when the sound/gesture was passed randomly?

- Did your thinking or feelings change as the game progressed?

- How can we use the lessons learned from this game to help us become more spontaneous at work?

Warm Up #5
Barney

Description
Ask players to name three things that begin with the same letter.

Goals
- To heighten ability to be spontaneous.
- To experience a non-judgmental atmosphere.
- To strengthen the ability to be flexible.
- To operate within ambiguity.

Number of Participants
Unlimited

Time
10-15 minutes, depending on number of participants

Materials
None

Process
Have the group form a circle.

Introduce the goals of the game.

Start the game by standing in the middle of the circle. "I'm going to point to a player at random and call out a letter. When I do, you come up with the name of a person, an object or service that can be sold and a location, all beginning with letter I call out. For example, let's say I call out the letter 'F.' The player I point to might respond with 'Frank sells fish in Finland.'"

The players continue the game, as you throw letters randomly at the people in the circle. If at any time a player can't come up with a response, that player becomes the caller and takes your place in the center of the circle You can join the game or remain in the observer role.

Suggested Questions for Debrief

- How satisfied are you with your participation? In what way were you dissatisfied with the answers you came up with? Can you relate that sense of dissatisfaction to any specific instances at work?

- What were thinking if you became the caller? How does this relate to your perception of your role in a team building situation?

- In what way was this game fun?

- In what way was this game stressful? What parallels can you draw between the stressors of this game and the stressors of work?

- How is being able to move forward in spite of ambiguity helpful in your day to day work?

Beyond the Warm Up

Warm ups kick off a learning session. Now it's time to explore and experience the power of improvisation.

Let go.

Have fun.

Emjoy the moment!

The Alphabet Story

Description
Players build a scene using all 26 letters of the alphabet, in order.

Goals
- To build concentration and listening skills.
- To enhance spontaneity and creativity.
- To accept from others.
- To hone flexibility.

Number of Participants
Works best with 5-10 players.

Time
20-30 minutes

Materials
None, although you may want to suggest an arena for a story, especially if working with people who don't have much experience with improvisation. It also helps to have a small bell available in case you need to stop and refocus the game.

Process
Introduce the goals of the game.

Tell the group, "You're going to be telling a story in 26 sentences. The story must make sense. Who'd like to volunteer to start our story?"

Set the scene. (Example: "You are at a wedding. You are all friends and/or family of either the bride or the groom. The groom is standing at the altar and the bride is a no show." Or "You're a giant who's come to Cincinnati to visit the Rock 'n Roll Hall of Fame.")

"I want you to make up a story about the giant going to the Rock 'n Roll Hall of Fame, using all the letters of the alphabet, in order. I'm going to choose the letter 'R' to start the story. Begin." The person who volunteered to start our story offers up the first line of the story, beginning with the letter "R".

"Rock and roll was the giant's favorite music."

The volunteer then chooses another player, who will continue the story, starting his or her sentence with the letter "S".

"So he decided to go visit the Rock and Roll museum and flew to Cincinnati on the back of his favorite dragon."

That player then points to another in the group, who begins his or her line with "T"- "To his surprise, the dragon informed the giant that since it was winter, he would need a cask of dragon brandy in order to get through the trip." That player then points to another participant, who begins his or her line with the letter "U" - "Unbelievable," the giant exclaimed. "I can't believe what I have to do just to get this dragon to do my bidding!"

The story continues through all 26 letters of the alphabet, ending on the letter "Q."

Reminders
This game can get bogged down if the participants are listening to their inner critics. You can try giving each person 5 seconds to begin their sentence. If they don't, ring a bell and have the previous speaker choose another player.
If you sense the story going off track, remind the players that the story must make sense.

Suggested Questions for Debrief

- What did you think of the story the team created?

- What was difficult about the game?

- What was easy for you?

- How did you feel when the bell rang during your turn?

- What changes did you notice in your body/breathing during the game?

- Did you have an idea of what you wanted to say but then couldn't make it fit by the time the story came to you? How did you respond? How does that response mirror your actions at work when circumstances, co-workers or a boss impact your work?

- What did you think about having to alter the direction you wanted to take the story? Do you experience these same thoughts when called upon to change course at work?

- What were you thinking/feeling when you passed off the story to someone else?

- How did it feel to have your contribution to the story acknowledged?

- What can this game teach us about flexibility in the workplace?

- What experiences can we take from this game and apply to our day to day work life?

*Thanks to colleague Martha Legare for her dragon contribution.

Sixty Second Life

Description
Participants introduce one another to the group.

Goals
- To break down barriers and build trust.
- To build effective listening skills.
- To create more collaborative teams.

Number of Participants
6-20 (in even numbers)

Time
15-25 minutes (depending on number of participants)

Materials
None.

Process
Have everyone pair off.

Introduce the goals of the game.

Have each duo decide who will be "A" and who will be "B".

"I'm going to give each of you one minute to interview your partner. At the end of the interview, you're going to introduce your partner to the rest of the group.

"A's begin."

At the end of a minute, have each "A" introduce their partner to the group. Repeat the exercise, with each "B" interviewing their

"A" partner for one minute, and then introduce the partner to the whole group.

Suggested Questions for Debrief

- How comfortable did you feel interviewing your partner? Being interviewed?

- In what way did knowing you'd be introducing your partner to the group impact how you listened?

- How did you feel sharing things about yourself with your partner?

- In what ways did you censor yourself? How did knowing that the information might be shared with the whole group impact what information you shared?

- What similarities did you discover between yourself and other members of the group?

- How has your thinking about the group changed? What does this exercise teach us about how to build stronger, more trusting relationships?

- How can we use the experience of this exercise to help us explore issues at work?

A Change of Hat

Description
Players create a story based on a scenario. The hats they wear identify their characters. As they switch hats, they switch characters.

Goals
- To listen to understand.
- To be spontaneous and hone creativity.
- To let go and accept the ideas of others.
- To experience flexibility.

Number of Participants
3-4

Time
10-15 minutes

Materials
You'll need a selection of hats that easily convey a character. Plan on having at least a dozen available. Examples: a fireman's helmet, a sailor cap, a baseball cap, a cowboy hat, a beret, a pirate's hat, a nurse's cap, a hairnet, a swim cap, a motorcycle helmet, a swim cap.

You can have a selection of scenarios in mind – a family on a car trip and their vehicle breaks down, climbing the last leg of Mount Kilimanjaro, competing in an on-air cooking competition like "Chopped" or exploring the crash site of an unidentified flying object. You can also let the participants come up with scenarios. If you decide to take scenario ideas from the players, do so before you fully describe the game.
Hint: An easy way for either you or participants to come up with scenarios is to take stories that are well-known in a new di-

rection. For example, you come upon Little Red Riding Hood and she's gotten the better of the wolf.

Process
Introduce the goals of the game.

Ask for volunteers.

"Now, I want each of you to choose a hat and put it on. You're going to create a story based on a scenario, and you'll be identified as specific characters by the hat you're wearing."

Tell the players that when you say "Freeze," they're to stop telling the story. During the "freeze", you'll switch the hats around (you can change one or all the hats at the same time) and when you say "Story", the players are to continue telling their story in the voice of the character whose hat they now wear.

Remind the group that the story must make sense.

Note: You want to listen for both "yes and" and "yes but" statements. It's as important to "catch" participants doing it right and give them positive feedback.

Suggested Questions for Debrief

- What did you think of the story that was created?

- What did you think when you were forced to continue the story with someone else's character creation? How might these thoughts mirror what happens in a work situation when you don't have total control over a project?

- In what ways did you make the character "fit" your concept of what the character should be? In what way might you find yourself doing the same thing in a work situation?

- How frustrated did you become when you had to change hats?

- What does this game teach us about empathy and seeing a situation through another's perspective?

- How does acknowledging another's point of view help us in collaborating?

- How can we apply what we experienced in this game to our day to day work?

Rescue Me

Description
Players "rescue" one another from while singing a song.

Goals
- To sharpen listening skills.
- To build trust among members of a work team.
- To enhance spontaneity and creativity.
- To experience being a supportive member of a team.

Number of Participants
4-10

Time
10-15 minutes, depending upon the number of participants

Materials
None

Process
Have participants stand in a circle.

Introduce the goals of the game.

Ask for a volunteer to kick off the game, "I need one player to step into the center of the circle. You're going to start singing a song…any song. I want the rest of you to play close attention. As soon as our player in the middle shows signs of stopping (because they don't know any more of the lyrics, for example), another one of you needs to step forward, tap the singer on the shoulder and take their place. Then you start to sing a song that's inspired by our first singer's choice. Here's an example."

First singer: Sunshine on my shoulders makes me happy.

Second singer: You are my sunshine, my only sunshine. You make me happy, when skies are gray. You'll never know, dear, how much I love you.
Third singer: Only love can break a heart. Only love can mend it again.
Fourth singer: Silver threads and golden needles cannot mend this heart of mine.

The game ends when the group can no longer sustain it.

Tips
People can really have fun with this game….if they'll take part in it. Getting up in front of people is often challenging enough – asking them to sing may prove to be too much. Only you will know whether or not your group is ready for it.

Variations
You can play this game using a story rather than a song. Players "rescue" the storyteller when it appears the storyteller is having trouble continuing the story. This will take care of the added nervousness a group may feel at having to "sing" in front of others.

Suggested Questions for Debrief

- What made you tap into the game?

- What kept you from tapping into the game?

- How did these actions echo decisions you make at work on whether or not to get involved/contribute to a project?

- Did it take longer for people to tap into the game than you anticipated?

- How does this game build trust among team members?

- What feelings of vulnerability and risk did you experience during this game?

- How did you feel when you could see that a participant was struggling? Can you relate this to feelings you may have for a co-worker who's struggling with a project?

- What has this game taught us about group dynamics? What happened to the group as the exercise progressed? Did its dynamics change? How?

- What does this game tell us about the importance of everyone's participation when it comes to work teams?

Lines from a Hat

Description
Players create a scene, incorporating lines drawn from a hat.

Goals
- To experience accepting from others.
- To hone listening skills.
- To enhance flexibility.
- To sharpen creativity.

Number of Participants
4-6

Time
10-15 minutes

Materials
Paper, pencils and a hat, flower pot or some fun container.

Process
Have everyone take 3 or 4 small pieces of paper. Have them write one sentence on each piece of paper. Put all of these pieces into your hat (or other fun container).

Introduce the goals of the game.

Ask for volunteers to play the game. Tell the players they will create a scene, based on suggested relationships (i.e. they're all siblings). You can provide the relationship as facilitator or ask for suggestions from other participants.

As they play out the scene, members of the "audience" (those participants not taking part in the scene) periodically call out "line", at which time one member of the scene must draw a line from the hat and incorporate it into the scene. The line must be used verbatim and the scene should continue to make sense.

Reminders

You may need to remind the players to go back to their POC if they seem to lose their way. (Remember, the POC is the point of concentration – what the scene is about.) Remind the players how they are related and that their goal is to create a scene that makes sense.

Remind them to use the lines exactly as written.

Suggested Questions for Debrief

- What did you learn about your ability to be flexible? How can you draw on an ability to be flexible at work?

- Is there an advantage to having to use what's written without hesitation or discussion? In other words, what advantages do you see to moving ahead with an idea rather than judging it? How would this approach benefit brainstorming sessions?

- How frustrating was it to have to include the lines from others in the story?

- What was most satisfying about this game?

- What was least satisfying?

- As an observer, what emotions did you feel coming from the story tellers? What helped you pick up on non-verbal cues? How can we use non-verbal cues in strengthening our ability to community in the workplace?

- How can we use the concept of accepting ideas from others in a constructive way at work?

- What insights can you draw about your organization from this exercise?

Conducted Story

Description
Participants create a single story from short segments.

Goals
- To help strengthen our ability to see how every single person contributes to overall success.
- To build more collaborative teams.
- To practice moving ahead in the face of ambiguity.
- To develop ease with letting go of outcomes.

Number of Participants
4-6 plus a conductor

Time
10-20 minutes

Materials
None

Process
Ask for volunteers. Have them face the audience in a semi-circle.

Introduce the goals of the game.

Ask the audience to call out the name of a story they've never heard before but would like to hear now. ("Papa Wore a Red Dress and Sneakers.") Tell the participants, "You're going to create a story titled "Papa Wore a Red Dress and Sneakers" and we need each of you to help tell the story. I'm going to be the conductor. When I point to one of you, you'll start the story. And you'll keep going until I point to another member of our story telling team. They'll pick up where the last player stopped. If the previous player stopped in mid-word, the current player should pick up by finishing the word and then continuing with the story. I'll continue to choose new people to pick up the story and continue it. "

Participants should not try and plan ahead. They have no idea when the conductor will call on them. They may be called upon more than once. And the story will no doubt take some unexpected turns. Remind participants to pay attention so that they can continue to create a story that makes sense.

Variations:
Repeat the exercise and have one of the audience members be the conductor.
Choose a story topic that's specifically related to the company, organization or group you're working with. (For example, incorporating the challenges faced by a company that is downsizing or the success an organization is having in terms of retention.)

Suggested Questions for Debrief

- What did you think of the story you created as a team?

- What behaviors helped your ability to "jump into" the story effectively? What behaviors hindered that ability?

- Were you able to remain "in the moment" or did you find yourself planning ahead? What impact do you think either had?

- How would you assess your overall contribution to the story? How can we relate this to our thoughts about our overall contributions at work?

- How can we transfer our ability to move forward in this story, not knowing how it will turn out, to our ability to move forward when it comes to ambiguity in the workplace?

- How frustrating was it to let go of the story you wanted to tell? How freeing was it? What parallels can we draw about our experiences in the workplace when we have to "let go"?

- How can the experience of this game help us become more effective and collaborative team members?

Source: I came across this game in the book, "Playing Along" by Izzy Gesell. I included the debrief questions I ask when using this exercise.

Draw Person aka Paired Drawing

Description
Two participants create a portrait.

Goals
- To experience building on offers from others.
- To enhance collaboration.

Number of Participants
Unlimited, in groups of two

Time
5-10 minutes

Materials
Paper and pens.

Process
Have everyone pair off.

Introduce the goals of the game.

Have the duo choose who will start the drawing. "Okay, start by drawing one feature of a face. It can be any feature you want. Eye, nose, mouth, anything. The second player then adds another feature to the face. The two of you continue drawing a face together, alternating back and forth, contributing one line or feature at a time.

"I want you to work silently. Resist the urge to discuss the picture you're creating. Whenever you lift your pen from the paper, your turn is over and the other player takes over.

"When one of you hesitates to draw, the picture is finished."

When the picture is finished, have the two artists title it, alternating one letter at a time.

Suggested Questions for Debrief

- How easy did you find this game?

- In what ways did you find yourself blocking your partner's addition to the drawing?

- In what ways did you find your partner blocking your additions to the drawing?

- What were you thinking or how did you feel when your contribution to the drawing was blocked or altered?

- What were you thinking or how did you feel when your contribution to the drawing was accepted and enhanced?

- What does this tell us about the climate in which we work? Do you feel like your ideas are accepted? If so, how is that reflected in your behavior?

- If you think your ideas aren't valued at work, how do you react?

- How do you think your drawing would have been different if you had drawn it on your own?

- What experiences can we take from the game and apply to building collaboration with others at work?

Goal on One Side

Description
Two participants create a scene. One of them may speak, the other responds non-verbally.

Goals
- To enhance listening skills.
- To hone awareness of non-verbal communication.
- To experience building on the offers of others.

Number of Participants
Unlimited, in groups of two

Time
3-5 minutes

Materials
None

Process
Ask for two volunteers. Give them a scenario (i.e. a mother and daughter out shopping, a couple looking at a house to buy) and give one of the participants a goal. "One of you wants to buy this house and has to convince the other to go along with buying it. Only one of you can speak. The other may only communicate non-verbally." Note: The goal can be given to either the participant who speaks verbally or communicates non-verbally.

The game continues until the goal is met or 5 minutes is up.

Variations
Have the participants change tasks midway through the game. The original speaker goes silent and the silent player now speaks.

Try the scene with both participants using only non-verbal communication.

Suggested Questions for Debrief

- What kind of non-verbal signals did you pick up from your partner? What communication cues can we use besides words?

- Which of those non-verbal signals did you rely on more? Were there any that you ignored?

- As the non-speaker, in what ways were you frustrated in trying to communicate your needs?

- As the non-speaker, what changes did you make to clarify your desires?

- How easy was it for the observers to "read" the non-verbal participant?

- Did the observers notice anything non-verbal that the speaker ignored? How did you feel when that happened?

- How can we use non-verbal communication and our awareness of it in our everyday work lives?

- Was it clear when you met your goal?

- How different was it to communicate non-verbally rather than verbally?

- What conclusions can we draw from the experiences in this game regarding the need for effective communication that goes beyond words in both our personal and professional lives?

What's on Your List?

Description
Participants learn to be flexible thinkers while maintaining a logical conversation.

Goals
- To encourage more flexible thinking.
- To experience and become more comfortable with letting go of preconceived ideas.
- To build the ability to be spontaneous.

Number of Participants
2 participants at a time, plus an emcee

Time
5-10 minutes; limit each round to no longer than 2 minutes

Materials
An easel and markers, or paper and pencil. (Only the emcee will need to have the "shopping list".)

Process
Ask for two volunteers. Ask them to step away, out of earshot of the audience, so that the audience can put together a shopping list.

Ask the audience to then make a shopping list of 10 to 20 items. Make the list a mixture of ordinary and unusual items. For example, the list might include apples, a bag of manure, a raincoat, ground beef, a dog's squeak toy and a shower curtain.

Invite the volunteers back into the room. "Take a place in front of the audience. Then decide which one of you will start a conversation and, when you're ready, begin.

"I'll interrupt you at random and call out one of the items from the shopping list (apples). When you, Player 1, hear the word "apples", you need to mention "apples" within the conversation as soon as possible. As soon as Player 1 mentions "apples", Player 2 picks up the conversation. I'll continue to interrupt at any time and call out another item from the list (a bag of manure) and now Player 2 incorporates 'bag of manure' into the conversation. Player 1 now picks up the conversation again. I'll continue to interrupt and you will continue to have your conversation until all items on the list have been added to the conversation."

Here's an example of how the conversation might go:

Player 1: "If an apple a day keeps the doctor away, I'm going to start eating two apples a day."

Player 2: "I had an aunt who ate a dozen crab apples a day. The tree was loaded with fruit because she spread a bag of manure around its roots every three days."

Player 1: "I'm allergic to manure. Whenever my parents took me to ride ponies, they made me wear a raincoat to keep manure dust from blowing on me."

Player 2: "I bet it was one of those bright yellow slickers. They remind me of a school bus. My dog used to chase the school bus every morning until I got him a squeak toy shaped like a bright yellow school bus. "

Variation: You can create a shopping list of items that are relevant to the specific participants or to an organization. For example, if you're working with an IT group, your list might include jump drive, Google glass, RAM, Bluetooth, Wi-Fi, charger, compact disc, ear buds, jawbone and Smart watch. A team within a health care organization might have a list that includes latex gloves, goggles, stethoscope, speculum, cotton, defibrillator, gauze, syringes, scrubs and tourniquet.

Suggested Questions for Debrief

- How uncomfortable were you, not knowing what was on the list?

- What was your discomfort level in worrying how you would incorporate the item into the conversation?

- What can the experience of this exercise uncover about our ability to be flexible?

- At any point, did you feel the need to censor yourself? Why?

- In what ways did you feel pressured to react spontaneously?

- How can we use the concept of being flexible to our advantage at work? In life?

- How can the experience of this game help us continue to move forward even when we're unsure of outcomes? How is moving forward in the face of ambiguity helpful at work? In life?

The Way I See It

Description
Participants share their perception of the kind of work environment they'd like to experience on a daily basis. It's their "preferred future."

Goals
- To practice speaking up.
- To build trust.
- To enhance team building and collaboration.
- To surface challenges.

Number of Participants
3-15

Time
10 – 20 minutes

Materials
Flip chart and markers

Process
Have everyone sit in a circle. Provide a specific focus for the group's visioning. For example, it might be "How will you describe your team three months from now?" or "In what ways will your team impact the organization's success?"

"Okay, everyone close your eyes. I want you to take a moment and think about how you'd like to be able to describe this team three months from now.

"We all want to hear your preferred vision of how this team will work together in the future.

"When you're ready, share your vision with the group. You can use one word or a short sentence. Share one thought at a time – wait for at least one other team member to share their vision before sharing another one of yours.

"Begin when you're ready."

Note: As the facilitator, jot down participant responses on the flip chart for later discussion. I've used this exercise for teams that are newly formed, those that are under-performing and those that are working well together and want a "check-in" to make sure they remain in alignment with mission and vision. Some of the responses I've gotten include:

- "No one's afraid to speak up."
- "Everybody listens to everybody else."
- "Every idea gets a 'look-see'."
- "We trust each other."
- "We've got each other's backs."

Let the exercise come to a natural conclusion, ending when participants have nothing further to say.

Note: It's not unusual for participants to share negative things that are currently going on within the team, especially if the team is under-performing. Simply stop the exercise and remind participants that the goal of the game is to envision their idea of what an effective team looks like in the future and to share that vision.

Also, if you're working with a team that's only been together a short time, has been buffeted by recent rapid change or is perceived by the organization or its leader as distrustful, under-performing and/or in distress, try an exercise like "Sixty Second Life" (page 101) with the team before embarking on "The Way I See It." The former provides an opportunity for team members to begin breaking down barriers and develop trust by getting to know one another as individuals.

Suggested Questions for Debrief

- In what ways was it hard for you to speak up during this exercise? In what ways did it become easier?

- If you are uncomfortable speaking up during team meetings, what roadblocks were removed for you during this exercise?

- How can the experience of this exercise change our perception about speaking up during team meetings?

- How does the experience of this exercise influence how we view the need for everyone to contribute?

- What changed for you as a group during the exercise? What happened to the group's dynamic?

- As a result of this exercise, how might the group function differently in the future?

- Looking at the shared vision of what a future team would look like, what are three things the team will commit to do from this day forward to bring this vision to reality?

This is not a Rope

Description
Participants use a rope to explore options.

Goals
- To encourage new ways of looking at the familiar.
- To sharpen the ability to see things from a different perspective.
- To enhance creativity.

Number of Participants
6-12

Time
10-15 minutes

Materials
A 4 foot piece of rope

Process
Have everyone stand in a circle. Place a four feet length of rope in the center of the circle. (If you have a large group, you can make several circles. You can either use a rope in each of these circles or introduce another everyday object, like a roll of paper towels or a baking pan.)

Introduce the goals of the game.

Ask participants to step forward, take the rope and see it as something else (i.e. This is not a rope. This is a snake.). As the participant names it, have them demonstrate what it does. (For the snake, they could make it slither on the ground.) Have the player put the rope back into the center of the circle.

Suggestions

As the game progresses, it will become more difficult to come up with ideas. Have the players try picking up the rope and playing with it – this can help trigger ideas. You should also have in mind a number of things the rope could be so you can help jump start the game if it gets bogged down.

Suggested Questions for Debrief

- As children we could easily transform everyday objects into something else. In what ways is it more difficult to do this as adults?

- In what ways did moving the rope help you see new possibilities for its use?

- At any point, did you feel the need to censor yourself? Why?

- In what ways did you feel pressured to see the rope as something else?

- If you didn't take part in the game, what held you back?

- How can we use the concept of seeing something familiar in a different light at work? In everyday life?

- How can the experience of this game help us become more effective problem solvers?

Sell This
aka Spontaneous Marketing

Description

Small groups invent a name, log line, logo and ad campaign and pitch it to everyone. For example, participants may decide they're a group of engineers who've invented a new mountain bike. They name the new bike the Peak Experience. Their log line or tag line might be "the perfect way to get that mountain high".

Goals

- To sharpen creativity.
- To accept and build on the offers of others.
- To enhance collaboration.
- To hone communication skills.

Number of Participants

Unlimited, divided into small groups of 3-5 players

Time

15-20 minutes; allow 3 minutes for each group to share their campaigns

Materials

A flip chart for each group.
Paper and markers.
Stop watch for facilitator.

Process

Divide the larger group into smaller, equal groups of 3-5 players. Give each group paper, flip chart and markers.

Introduce the goals of the game.

"Each group has 15 minutes to come up with a name, a logo, a logline and an ad campaign to market your group. When time is up, each group will share their campaign with everyone."

Emphasize that each member of a group is expected to take part in their presentation.

Facilitator's Note:
Give the group an update on time every 3 minutes. Suggest they move on to another component of the ad campaign if they find themselves stuck.

Variation:
Have each group put together a marketing plan for a new product that their organization may be rolling out, for example, a new computer software program.

Suggested Questions for Debrief

- Did everyone think there was equal participation between group members?

- What were you thinking if you hesitated to offer up suggestions?

- What comparisons can you draw between censoring yourself during the game and not speaking up at work?

- What was the most difficult part of this game?

- Were there times you felt yourself blocking suggestions from other team members rather than accepting them? How did this affect your ability to move forward as a group?

- Were there times when you thought your suggestions were being blocked by fellow team members? How did that affect your decision to continue to offer ideas?

- How did being under a time constraint affect your contributions?

- How satisfied are you with the campaign your team created?

- What experiences can we take from this game and apply to our collaborative efforts at work?

- What experiences can we take from this game and apply to our everyday lives?

Innovate or Die

Description
Players find as many new uses for an object as possible.

Goals
- Enhance the ability to think "outside the box".
- Practice saying "yes and".
- Hone the ability to see things in a new perspective.
- Learn to accept the offers of others.

Number of Participants
Unlimited, divided into teams of 4-5

Time
15 minutes, plus 3 minutes for each group to present their ideas

Materials
Paper, pens, flip charts and markers.

Process
Divide the group into smaller groups of 4 or 5 players.

Introduce the goals of the game.

"Each of you works for the Impossible Mission Force. The Rubber Band Man Company has just learned that an overseas company has developed a new product that will make rubber bands obsolete. In order to survive, the Rubber Band Man Company needs to develop new practical uses for rubber bands and the company's hired your group to come up with those uses.

"Each of your groups has 15 minutes to generate as many ideas as you can for uses of the rubber band.

"At the end of 15 minutes, I'm going to ask each group to share your ideas with everyone."

Tip

Before you start the game, it may be helpful to provide the following from creativity consultant Mel Donaghue:

D -   Don't judge the ideas.
O -   Outrageous ideas are desirable.
V -   Volume and Variety in ideas are needed.
E -   Extend and Elaborate on others' ideas.

Also, listen carefully for blocking in "yes but" comments.

Suggested Questions for Debrief

- In what ways did your inner critic affect your participation in the brainstorming session?

- What behaviors did you use to overcome your inner critic?

- In what ways did you notice your ability to "think outside the box" change as the game progressed?

- In what ways did working with a group enhance your ability to problem solve?

- In what ways did working with a group hinder your ability to problem solve?

- How did it feel to accept and build on the ideas presented by other members of your group?

- How did it feel to have your own ideas accepted and built upon by other members of your group?

- What behaviors contributed to the success of this game? What behaviors hindered the success of this game?

- How can we apply what we experienced in this game to brainstorming sessions we have at work?

Yes, And

Description
Players tell a story by agreeing with what the other players say, no matter what.

Goals
- Experience the concept of accepting from others.
- Explore the golden rule of improvisation.
- Hone your ability to listen to understand.
- Enhance your ability to pick up on non-verbal communication.

Number of Participants
Unlimited, in groups of 3 or 4

Time
3-5 minutes per story

Materials
None

Process
Ask for volunteers.

Introduce the goals of the game.

Ask the "audience" to suggest the relationship between our participants. (They could be family members on a car trip, strangers at a baseball game, workers waiting to hear about a new contract, strangers in a dog obedience class.)

Ask one player to start a conversation with a positive, declarative statement (for example, player 1 starts the story with "I'm looking forward to seeing Old Faithful"), keeping in mind her/his relationship to the other players. Player 2 agrees with player 1 by saying, "Yes and…" and then contributes to the conversation. Player 3 then responds to player 2 in the same fashion, and player 4 responds to player 3, also using the "yes and" format. Continue the story until its natural conclusion.

Reminder

It's important for each player to say "yes and" before adding their own declarative sentence to the story. The use of "and" helps the players naturally open the story to possibilities. Some participants may find it awkward to start each sentence with the actual words "Yes and." This awkwardness may stifle participants. Try letting them substitute words like "okay," "great," "alright" or "you bet" for "yes."

Suggested Questions for Debrief

- How satisfied were you with the story you created?

- In what ways did saying "yes and" out loud help in breaking down obstacles to agreement?

- What did you think or how did you feel knowing that what you said would be accepted by others?

- What did you think or how did you feel knowing that you had to accept what others offered?

- What value is there in creating a story/scenario together? How can we relate this value to our everyday work experiences?

- In what ways can you use the "yes and" principle in your work? In everyday life?

- What were you thinking as you watched the story unfold? What parallels might we draw between this story and watching a work project unfold?

Add a Word
aka One Word at a Time

Description
Players make up a story, one word at a time.

Goals
- Elevate your ability to react spontaneously.
- Reinforce the importance of process in achieving a goal. Strengthen your comfort in relying on others.
- Experience working towards a common goal.
- Experience letting go of control.

Number of Participants
Works best with groups of no more than 15

Time
15 minutes

Materials
None

Process
If you have a large group, ask for 10-15 volunteers. Have them face the "audience". If there's no "audience", have the players form a circle.

Introduce the goals of the game.

"You're going to create a story together, a story that's never been told before. And you're going to create this story one word at a time."

Ask the "audience" to suggest a title for the story. If there is no "audience", then take suggestions from the players. Take the very first suggestion you hear. This gives you an opportunity to model the concept of accepting whatever is offered from others. Should someone suggest a real story title like "Little Red Riding Hood," accept the title and then build on it by asking for an elaboration on the story, something like "Little Red Riding Hood Gets the Best of the Big Bad Wolf."

> Choose a player to start the story. As you move around from player to player, each will add one word to the story until it's complete.
>
> **Reminders**
> Remind the players to be spontaneous in their responses. They should try to keep from anticipating what they'll add to the story as it comes their way.
>
> Remind the group that there are no wrong words to add to the story. This is a new story that no one's ever heard before so any words we add will be alright.
>
> If the story bogs down, you can stop and start a new story. Doing so doesn't indicate failure, only that we're opening the door to a new possibility.
>
> **Variation**
> Try this game with two players, each one offering one word at a time.
>
> **Suggested Questions for Debrief**
>
> - What did you think of the story your team created?
>
> - What did you find hardest about taking part in this game?

- What did you find easiest about taking part in this game?

- In what ways did the game become easier the more you played?

- What did you think about your own contributions?

- What insights did you have about your ability to "let go" of an end result?

- How might this ability to "let go" enhance your capabilities at work?

- What caused the game to bog down?

- What does the experience of this game show us about the value of not making a plan, but rather "staying in the moment"?

- What conclusions can we draw from this game about the importance of every team member to the effectiveness of a work team?

- What conclusions can we draw about how blocking the contributions of others can negatively affect a team?

Awareness Quiz

Description
Participants pair off and have a conversation. Suggest that they pair off with either someone they don't know, or someone they don't know well.

Goals
- To enhance listening skills.
- To amplify an ability to take in non-verbal cues.
- To discover how our inner critic affects our ability to break down barriers.

Number of Participants
Unlimited, in teams of two

Time
5-10 minutes

Materials
None

Process
Have the players pair up.

Introduce the goals of the game.

Have the players engage in a short conversation. You may want to suggest a topic – for example, find out three things they have in common.

After 3-4 minutes, end the conversations and have the players stand back to back with their eyes closed.

"I'm now going to give you a quiz. Think about the answers – don't say them out loud."

Ask the following questions:

What kind of shoes is your partner wearing? Color? Are they wearing socks? What color?

What are they wearing from the waist down? Color? Material? Are they wearing a belt?

What are they wearing from the waist up? Color? What kind of neckline does it have? How does it fasten?

Are they wearing jewelry? What kind?

What about their hair? The style? The color? How long?

Are they wearing glasses? What color are they?

Okay, open your eyes and face each other.

Suggested Questions for Debrief

- How did you do? Anyone get 100%? Anyone get nothing?

- What kinds of things did you notice? Why? If you filled in details about your partner that aren't there, what does this tell us about the mind's ability to fill in the blanks when memory fails us? How does this knowledge impact or help us in our day to day lives?

- Why do we block out so much information?

- How do we decide what to pay attention to?

- What impact, if any, did it have that I said I was going to give you a quiz?

- How much better would you have done if I had asked you to study the person ahead of time?

- What does the experience of this game tell us about our powers of observation?

- What do you wish you'd done differently?

- How can we improve our levels of awareness?

- How can our ability to take in non-verbal cues help us in everyday work and life situations?

Source: I was first turned on to this game by a friend years ago, when he was asked to do this with a partner while undergoing couples' therapy. I then ran across this more sophisticated version adapted from Patricia Ryan, improv instructor, Stanford University and David K. Reynolds, Ph.D.

Tag-a-Word

Description
Two sets of players tell a story. Each set is made up of a primary story teller and a partner.

Goals
- To enhance spontaneity.
- To build creativity.
- To experience accepting offers from others.
- To experience being part of a team.

Number of Participants
Two per game

Time
3-5 minutes

Materials
None

Process
Ask for 2 volunteers.

Introduce the goals of the game.

Have the players decide who will be the main storyteller and who will be the partner. Give the players a relationship and a task to complete. (Example: they're movers and have to move a grand piano from a second floor apartment.)

"The two of you are going to create a story together. Whenever the person you've chosen as the main storyteller draws a blank, s/he can tap his/her partner, who then shouts out the first word that comes to mind. The main storyteller must then use that word to continue the scene, justifying its use in the context of the story."

Suggested Questions for Debrief

- How did you choose which player would be the main storyteller and which would be the partner?

- How did it feel knowing there was someone who would step in when you got stuck? Did that feeling change in any way as the game progressed?

- What did you think/feel when you needed to ask for help?

- What reasons can you give for not tapping your partner for help? How can we relate this to not using all members of a team at work?

- As partners, in what ways were you frustrated at not being in control of the story?

- What does the experience of this game teach us about individual contributions at work, even those that seem small?

- What did this game tell you about your function as a team member? As a team leader?

- What can the experience of this game teach us about how to build more effective teams?

Say What?

Description
Create a story using suggestions provided by others.

Goals
- To accept offers from others.
- To hone the ability to be flexible.
- To increase spontaneity.
- To enhance creativity.

Number of Participants
Unlimited, in groups of 3-6

Time
5-10 minutes

Materials
A flip chart or white board; marker

Process
Ask for 3-6 volunteers.

Introduce the goals of the game.

Take suggestions from the audience and fill in the following blanks: In a _____, with a _____, while _____. One example might be: In a frying pan, with a bull rider, while a tree is falling. (I gave an example of the kind of suggestions that usually come from observers. Typically, they try to provide suggestions that are anything but ordinary. In actuality, "ordinary" suggestions work out just fine. We're not concerned with trying to be funny, but rather with trying to connect and create something together that makes sense.)
Write several suggestions down where all the players can see them.

Ask the players to use these suggestions to create a story. "One of you can start the story. You can choose to begin the story with one of the suggestions on the board, or begin elsewhere and include the suggestions in the body of the story. You can use a suggestion separately or combine it with another. After you use the suggestion(s), point to another player, who'll continue the story, using suggestions that remain."

As suggestions are used, cross them off the board.

The game continues until all players and all suggestions have been used.

Suggested Questions for Debrief

- How did having these suggestions make it easier or harder to tell the story?

- How is having others focused on a shared outcome helpful? How can we relate that to our work as members of a team?

- Once you heard the suggestions, did you have an idea of how to build the story?

- What did you think when the story went in a direction that you hadn't anticipated? Can you relate to the same thing happening in a work situation?

- If you thought the story was going off track, did you try to change its direction? How? What parallels can you draw with getting off track at work?

- What does the experience of this game tell us about group dynamics?

- Observers, what were you thinking when you made the suggestions you did?

- What can we learn from the choices we make? How can we apply this to our everyday work lives?

- What experiences can we take from this game and apply to our understanding of what it takes to build an effective team?

- What can we learn from this game about becoming a better collaborator?

- How might the group function differently if we were to play this game again?

Carpooling

Description
Players take on each other's emotions during their carpool ride.

Goals
- To enhance ability to listen to understand and be aware of non-verbal behavior.
- To accept offers from others.
- To build rapport among team members.
- To hone flexibility.
- To enhance spontaneity.

Number of Participants
Unlimited, in groups of 4-5

Time
5-10 minutes

Materials
White board or flip chart, big cards on a string, markers

Process
Ask for volunteers.

Introduce the goals of the game.

Tell the group they're members of a carpool. Have the group choose a driver. One by one, they'll be picked up for work and dropped off somewhere along the way.

Assign each individual an emotion or attitude (Get suggestions from observers. Choose a variety, such as anger, joy, depression, anxiety, fear.)

Decide in what order our workers will be picked up and review the order and the emotions.

Note: It helps to write down the order in which workers will be picked up – do this so everyone can see the order. Or you can simply have the workers line up in the order in which they're going to be picked up.

Also, this isn't a memory game - I put big cards on a string which players can slip over their heads and wear like a bib. I leave the cards blank until we choose the emotions prior to the game.

Remind the group, "Whenever a new person is picked up, you must all take on that new person's emotion.

"After the last person has been picked up and you've played the scene for a brief while, that last person will be dropped off. When that player leaves, all of you in the carpool will revert to the previous emotion, until the next person leaves, and so on until the last person left is the driver, with his/her original emotion."

Reminders
When you play several rounds of this game, make sure you choose different emotions for each round.

Be prepared to coach the group as the drive to work continues. You may have to remind them that workers need to be picked up or dropped off. You may also have to remind them to reflect the emotion of their most recent passenger.

Variation
You can also use a meeting as the setting for this game. In this setting, players can enter, exit and re-enter the meeting

Suggested Questions for Debrief

- How does it feel to take on the emotions of others? In what ways does this affect our own behavior?

- In what ways was it difficult to assume the emotions of others? Are there some emotions that are more uncomfortable to assume than others? Why?

- In what ways is it helpful to be able to tune into or empathize with what others are feeling?

- How can we use emotions to influence certain events?

- In what ways is it helpful to use our emotions to influence others? In what ways can it be detrimental?

- What does the experience of this game tell us about which emotions may better serve us during team activities?

- What can we learn from experiencing this game about the importance of being able to empathize with our co-workers? With our leaders?

The Yada, Yada, Yada Interview
aka Gibberish Interview

Description
One player speaks in a nonsense language during a press conference. Another player translates his responses.

Goals
- To enhance spontaneity.
- To build creativity.
- To experience accepting offers from others.
- To sharpen ability to receive and process non-verbal communication.

Number of Participants
Unlimited, two at a time

Time
5-15 minutes

Materials
None

Process
Explain the concept of a nonsense language. It's sometimes referred to as gibberish. Because people new to the process of improvisation may get bogged down in trying to invent a language, suggest that players use a set phrase – like yada, yada, yada or blah, blah, blah – to serve as the nonsense language.

Ask for two volunteers. Have them decide which player will be the subject and which will be the translator.

Introduce the goals of the game.

Get suggestions from the audience on the relationship of the two players. For example, the one who speaks in a nonsense language may be a pitcher from Japan who's been signed to a professional contract for an American baseball team. The pitcher is meeting the press for the first time.

"Now, our observers (the audience) will ask questions of the person being interviewed. The interpreter will translate the questions into a nonsense language. And our interviewee will respond to the questions in a nonsense language, which our interpreter will then translate into English for our observers."

Note
Once participants are comfortable with the idea of using a nonsense language, they can try and create a language of their own.

Reminders
Be patient. Some business professionals may feel awkward when asked to speak in a made up language. Demonstrate gibberish often to encourage participation.

Keep in mind that there are no right answers in improvisation. Whatever either player says is okay.

Coach participants to answer every question with "yes" and then elaborate.

Variation
If someone in the group speaks a language that no one else in the group understands, have them use that in lieu of a nonsense language.

Suggested Questions for Debrief
- How difficult was it to communicate without words so that everyone could understand? What thoughts/feelings were provoked?

- Other than words, what communication tools did you use to try and relay your answers?

- Were there any communication cues that were easier to read than others? What were they?

- Did the translator correctly pass on what you were trying to say?

- As the translator, what difficulties did you encounter in trying to figure out what the subject was saying?

- What parallels can we draw with our ability to communicate with co-workers?

- Observers, how did the translation you received match the interpretation of the answers that you made in your heads? In what ways didn't the translation match?

- What can we learn from this game about the role of intonation, reflection and gestures in communication?

- What can we learn from this game about the role that non-verbal cues play in effective communication?

- What experiences can we take from this game and apply to our day-to-day work life?

Sculpt This!

Description
Players create living sculptures.

Goals
- To experience accepting from others.
- To enhance spontaneity.
- To build creativity.
- To experience being part of a team.

Number of Participants
No more than 20, evenly divided into 2 groups.

Time
15-20 minutes

Materials
None

Process
Introduce the goals of the game.

Divide the players into 2 groups of equal number. One set of players forms a circle in the middle of the room, facing outwards. Each member of the other set of players positions him/herself in front of one of the players already in the circle.

"Now, those of you on the inside circle are clay or stone, and those of you in the outside circle are sculptors. Each of you sculptors will do one thing to the lump of clay or stone in front of you and then move clockwise to the next piece of clay/stone. You'll now do one thing to the new sculpture. You'll continue to move around the circle until you're back in front of your original work.

"Once in front of your original work, name it and introduce it to the group."

Variation

Each statue is equipped with a voice chip that can say only one sentence. Have the sculptors switch on the voice chip at the end of their explanation so we can hear from the works of art.

Notes

This game offers an excellent opportunity to see who "plays nice". Sculptors who try to put their art pieces into positions that are uncomfortable or hard to hold are easy to spot. That behavior may belie how that individual works within a team.

Also, you'll want to make note if there are players who undo the work of other players and replace it with their own. Remind the sculptors that the golden rule of improv is still at work – it's "yes and", which means that they accept the work of the previous sculptors and add to it.

This may be a tougher sell to certain segments of the business population, so know your group before trying this one.

Suggested Questions for Debrief

- In what way did your sculpture resemble what you had pictured when you first started?

- What did you like about adding to someone else's work?

- What did you dislike about adding to someone else's work?

- In what ways was it easier to add to the sculpture when you first started? In what ways was it harder?

- In what ways was it easier to add to the sculpture as it neared completion? In what ways was it harder?

- What did you think/feel about others altering your vision?

- As the sculpture, how did it feel to let go and give in to someone else's vision? In what ways did you resist?

- What do you wish you'd done differently during the game?

- What can we learn from the experience of this game in terms of how to work in teams more effectively?

- What can we learn from the experience of this game about behaviors that can undermine team productivity?

Stop Action

Description
Players are interrupted as they tell a story. They add elements provided by the audience during the interruptions.

Goals
- To enhance flexibility.
- To experience accepting offers from others.
- To strengthen ability to be spontaneous.
- To elevate creativity.
- To enhance ability to listen.

Number of Participants
Two players and one coach

Time
5-10 minutes

Materials
None

Process
Ask for two volunteers to be the storytellers. Ask for a volunteer to be the coach.

Introduce the goals of the game.

"You two storytellers are going to be telling a story based on a suggestion from the audience. At any time as the story is unfolding, the coach can say 'Freeze' and ask the audience for another suggestion, like 'What does storyteller number one have in his/her hand?' At this point, the audience gives a suggestion and storyteller number one will have to incorporate that suggestion into the scene.

"The coach continues to say 'Freeze' during the telling of the story and ask for additional suggestions from the audience, which will then have to be incorporated into the story.

"Continue until the story reaches its natural conclusion."

Notes

Let the scene develop. If the coach stops the players too often, the game will become about the suggestions from the audience and not about the goals.

It helps if the players incorporate physical movement into the storytelling, as it gives the coach something to work with in asking the questions when s/he says "Freeze." For example, the story will bog down if the coach is left with questions like, "What is player two thinking?' rather than "What is player two picking up from the ground?".

You may have to remind the players that once something is incorporated into the story, it stays there, unless they have removed it. For example, if the coach asks the above question, "What is player two picking up from the ground?" and either player answers that it's a dog, the dog should remain in the scene unless the players rid the scene of the dog themselves. For example, the dog may run off, or one player may have been watching the dog for someone who comes back, etc.

Suggested Questions for Debrief

- How satisfied were you with the story you told?

- What was hardest about this game? What was easiest?

- What does this game teach us about the ability to be flexible? In what way is flexibility a positive competency in your work environment?

- What insights did you gain about yourself and letting go of end results? How can valuing the concept of process over end results enhance teamwork?

- In what ways was it frustrating to have the direction of your story altered by the coach's interruption and the audience's suggestion? How can we relate that sense of frustration to having to shift gears in the work environment?

- As the coach, what motivated you to freeze the game?

- As the audience, in what ways were your suggestions prompted by the story? In what ways were your suggestions preplanned? What does the experience of this game show us about responding in the moment?

- In what way does the experience of this game build trust and rapport among players, including the audience?

- How is the experience of this game useful in providing insight as to how we can better work together as a team?

Status Games

Status is about hierarchy, a "pecking order" if you will. And we establish our place in this "pecking order" in a variety of ways. It could be something as simple as wearing a pair of shades, which raises our status simply because others can't read any submission in our eyes.

In the workplace, it's important to be aware of status and have the ability to move easily and confidently up and down the status ladder. For example, if you and a colleague are going over a report together, it wouldn't be unusual to sit side by side to go over the data. This seating arrangement puts you on equal footing, status wise. But if you're relaying the data to a leader, chances are more likely that you'll sit across from one another in the leader's office – which puts the leader in a higher status position.

Being able to "pick up" accurately on status – and adjust accordingly – affects how we behave…and is key when it comes to being able to effectively connect with people from all levels within an organization.

In experimenting with these games, it's useful to remember that sometimes people are reluctant to play a character of high status. And sometimes…others like it too much!

Demonstrate Status

(I first played this game in an acting class with Dr. Martin Bennison – his source was Keith Johnstone.)

Description

Players mingle at a gathering, with half of the group displaying high status physical behaviors and the other half displaying low status behaviors. After a few minutes, the groups switch behaviors. (You might try choosing a venue where status may be more obvious – say at a state dinner at the White House or backstage after a concert to meet a famous musical star.)

Goals

- To experience different status levels.
- To enhance non-verbal communication.
- To heighten ability to listen to understand.

Number of Participants

6 – 100

Time

5-15 minutes

Materials

None

Process

Divide players into two groups.

Introduce the goals of the game. You may want to take time and have a short review of the physical and verbal behaviors that we associate with low and high status. (I've provided examples below; for an in-depth discussion of these behaviors, consult "Impro: Improvisation for the Theatre" by Keith Johnstone, pages 41-52.)

These are some of the behaviors we associate with high status behavior:
- Takes over the physical space. "Walks tall."
- Looks directly at someone when speaking to them.
- Speaks loudly and often.
- Approaches people directly, both verbally and physically.
- Keeps head still.
- Moves smoothly.
- Keeps hands away from face.
- Chooses to ignore others.

These are some of the behaviors we associate with low status behavior:
- Takes up as little space as possible, feeling entitled to use only so much space.
- Speaks softly, maybe hesitating before beginning to speak.
- Avoids eye contact.
- Moves awkwardly, sometimes with jerky movement.
- Approaches people in a roundabout way, both verbally and physically.
- Puts hands near face, as if to hide.

Assign one group to play low status and the other group to play high status.

"You're all attending a party. You all know one another and are glad to be at the party. Please feel free to talk and mingle with anyone you choose, no matter which status group they belong to."

After a few minutes, have the players switch status roles and mingle again.

Tips

You may have to remind the players about specific behaviors that identify each status group. Also, because a discussion of status can be tricky, make sure you allow plenty of time for participants to ask questions and discuss the concept.

Variation

This game is an overt demonstration of status and can serve as an introduction to the concept. If the group seems to have trouble at first, try having the whole group display high status behaviors. Then have the whole group display low status behaviors.

Suggested Questions for Debrief

- In what ways were you more comfortable in one status than the other? How did those feelings manifest themselves?

- What assumptions did you make about the people playing the status opposite of yours? How can those assumptions affect relationships with our co-workers?

- In what way was communication different when you were speaking to someone of your status as opposed to someone of the opposite status?

- How much did the physical manifestations of status affect your communication? What physical things did you find annoying about each status level? What physical things did you find appealing?

- What parallels can we draw from the experience of this game and the real world?

- In what ways does status figure into the interactions you have with co-workers? With leaders?

- What are some examples of status interactions in your job? In your life?

- What can the experience of this game teach us about how we view someone or something unfamiliar to us?

- What experiences can we take from this game and apply to building more effective relationships at work?

Pecking Order

Description
Players create a story as they try to interpret the status of the other players.

Goals
- To experience the concept of status.
- To enhance non-verbal communication.
- To heighten ability to interpret status behavior.

Number of Participants
6-10

Time
5-10 minutes

Materials
None

Process
Ask for 6-10 volunteers.

Introduce the goals of the game.

Have each player choose a number between 1 and the number of players in the game. (The number 1 is lowest in status.) "More than one of you may choose the same number. Don't share the number you've chosen with anyone."

Ask the audience to pick a location and activity for our players. For example, the participants are all related, either by birth or marriage, and they're celebrating an occasion at a fancy restaurant. "Your celebration is being interrupted by people at the table next to you. How do you deal with it?"

During the exercise be sure to coach participants to be mindful of their status and to model that status in ways that allow other players to correctly interpret it. For example, if a player has chosen a low status number, s/he might try to get someone else to intervene with the rowdy group at the next table. Someone else who has chosen a number indicating high status might very well address the people at the other table directly.

Suggested Questions for Debrief

- How easy or difficult was it to identify the status of other players?

- How was it difficult to convey the status you chose?

- What clues did you use to communicate your status to other players?

- What clues did you pick up to identify the status of other players?

- What difficulties arose when status was misunderstood? How can we see those difficulties echoed in the workplace?

- What impact did status have on your ability to communicate? What parallels can you draw in terms of your ability to communicate across many levels in your organization?

- What did you discover if several of you chose the same status?

- How can we use what we learned from the experience of this game to relate with more clarity to people with whom we work?

- How can we use what we learned from the experience of this game to relate with more clarity to members of our family?

- What did the experience of this game teach us about the importance of and the role that status plays in the workplace?

Card Status

Description
Each player chooses a card from a deck of cards. Without looking at it, they tape the card to their forehead so that everyone else can see the card. The players then create a scene together, treating each other with the status indicated by the cards.

Goals
- To experience the concept of status.
- To build non-verbal communication skills.
- To enhance awareness.

Number of Participants
8-10

Time
5-10 minutes

Materials
1 deck of playing cards
Tape

Process
Ask for volunteers.

Have each participant draw a card from the deck, making sure that there are a variety of numbers handed out, low to high. (aces are high, twos are low) Ask players to refrain from looking at their cards.

Introduce the goals of the game.

Have the players attach the playing cards to their foreheads with tape so that they are visible to everyone else in the room.

"You're all a party for XYZ network to introduce new fall shows to the advertisers. I want each of you to treat the other players in a way indicated by the status on the card on their forehead. How others treat you will give you clues as to your own status. As you put the clues together, you should take on the behaviors that are associated with that status."

After a few minutes of mingling, ask the players to line up in the order in which they think they belong.

Invite the players to look at their cards.

Tips
Status can be touchy. You may want to make it "less real" at first by choosing a location like the hollow tree where the Keebler elves work or a saloon in the old west. And make sure you take as much time as you need to answer questions and/or concerns.

Suggested Questions for Debrief

- Were you able to identify your status correctly? If not, why?

- What cues did you pick up that helped you identify your status?

- What cues did you give to others to help them identify their status?

- What changes did you notice in your behavior as you moved from higher to lower status and back again?

- Identify times when you felt uncomfortable.

- How did you feel when others behaved in ways that were contrary to their status?

- What assumptions did you make about people based on their status?

- How can we use what we've learned about status in our everyday dealings with others at work?

- Based on your experiences with the game, what changes might you make at work with regard to your perception of status? (Both your own and others.)

Additional Resources

In addition to the exercises I've provided in this Field Guide, I'm including some additional resources where you'll find even more improv games. Pick out a few and try them!

Applied Improvisation Zone
http://rationalmadness.wordpress.com/treasures/cats3000-applied-improvisation-page/

Improv Encyclopedia http://improvencyclopedia.org/games/

John Thrower: Improvisation Exercises
http://cloudcuckoo.co.uk/jonthrower/improv_ex.htm

NISE Network Improv Exercises
http://www.nisenet.org/catalog/tools_guides/improv_exercises

End Notes

[1] Wilson, Edward O., "Consilience: The Unity of Knowledge", (1998) New York: Vintage Books
[2] Gladwell, Malcolm. "blink: The Power of Thinking without Thinking", (2005) New York: Little, Brown and Company
[3] Adams, Celine. Making Businesspeople Funny. The Training Report. n/d
[4] Huffington Post, February 27, 2014
[5] Parry, Donna. Chief Learning Officer Magazine. June 5, 2014
[6] Pfeffer, Jeffrey and Sutton, Robert I., "The Knowing-Doing Gap", Harvard Business School Press, 2000, page 253
[7] Innovation Anarchy, January 29, 2013
[8] 9 Things Invented or Discovered by Accident, Publications International Ltd.
[9] Discovery Channel, n/d
[10] Yorton, Tom, "Using Improv Methods to Overcome the Fear Factor", Wiley Periodicals, January 14, 2005
[11] Silverthorn, Sean. "5 Personal Core Competencies for the 21st Century", CBS Moneywatch, August 13, 2009
[12] The Quotations Page
[13] Rosenberg, Michael, "The Flexible Thinker: A Guide to Creative Wealth", (1998) Orange You Glad Publishers
[14] Yorton, Tom. "8 Ways to Improvise Your Way to Success", Connect Magazine, April/May 2013
[15] Daniel, Katie. "Improvising Leadership: Finding Comfort in Ambiguity", Leadership Compass, n/d
[16] Friedman, Thomas L., "The World is Flat: A Brief History of the Twenty-First Century", (2005) New York: Farrar, Straus & Giroux
[17] "Schwinn Hits the Skids", Venture Navigator, August 2007
[18] Pfeffer, Jeffrey and Sutton, Robert I., "The Knowing-Doing Gap", (2000) New York: Harvard Business School Press
[19] Jobs, Steve and Wozniak, Steve, Newsletter, "A House Journal of IEEX", Vol. 11, #1, Jan-Mar 2002
[20] MacKenzie, Gordon. "Orbiting the giant hairball: A corporate fool's guide to surviving with grace." (1996) New York: Viking
[21] Goleman, Daniel. "Working with Emotional Intelligence", (1998) New York: Bantam Books
[22] Conklin, Robert. ThinkExist.com
[23] Guinon, Albert. The Quotation Page
[24] Faculty Commons: Speaking Across the Curriculum
[25] Kelley, Robert, Carnegie-Mellon University, Learning Technologies Conference, 2006
[26] Statistics for Making the Case, USAID, n/d
[27] Marmot, Michael, "The Status Syndrome: How Social Standing Affects Our Health and Longevity", (2004) New York: Henry Holt & Company

[28] Bennis, Warren. Creativity@Workquotes
[29] Fromm, Erich. Wisdom Quotes
[30] deBono, Edward, QuotesWorld.org
[31] Covey, Steven. About.com:quotations
[32] Boston Consulting Group, Senior Management Survey on Innovation, 2004-2005
[33] Sobel, Robert, "When Giants Stumble: Classic Business Blunders and How to Avoid Them", (1999) New Jersey: Prentice-Hall Press
[34] Ibid.
[35] Ibid.
[36] Ray, Michael and Myers, Rochelle, "Creativity in Business", (1989) New York: Bantam Dell
[37] Amabile, Teresa, "How to Kill Creativity", Harvard Business Review, Sept 1998
[38] Omidyar, Peter, eBay Press Release, Feb 24, 1999

Bibliography

Drucker, Peter. "The Age of Discontinuity: Guidelines to Our Changing Society", Harper & Row (1968)

Gelb, Michael J., "How to Think Like Leonardo da Vinci", Delacorte Press (1998)

Gezell, Izzy, "Playing Along", Whole Person Associates (1997)

Gladwell, Malcolm, "blink", Little, Brown and Company (2005)

Goleman, Daniel, "Working with Emotional Intelligence", Bantam Books (1998)

Johnstone, Keith, "Impro: Improvisation and the Theatre", A Theatre Arts Book (1981)

Lowe, Robert, "Improvisation, Inc.", Jossey-Bass/Pfeiffer (2000)

MacKenzie, G., "Orbiting the Giant Hairball", Viking, New York (2001)

Madson, Patricia Ryan, "Improv Wisdom", Bell Tower (2005)

Michalko, Michael, "Cracking Creativity", Ten Speed Press (2001)

Pfeffer, Jeffrey and Sutton, Robert I., "The Knowing-Doing Gap", Harvard Business School Press (2000)

Sobel, Robert, "When Giants Stumble", Prentice Hall Press (1999)

Spolin, Viola, "Improvisation for the Theatre", Northwestern University Press (1983)

Werner, David L., "Battling the Inner Dummy", Prometheus Books (1999)

Made in the USA
Middletown, DE
18 May 2015